Janice VanCleave's
Guide to More of the Best Science Fair Projects

John Wiley & Sons, Inc.

New York • Chichester • Weinheim • Brisbane • Singapore • Toronto

Dedication

It is a pleasure to dedicate this book to my friend and helpmate, my husband, Wade VanCleave

Acknowledgments

I wish to express my appreciation to these science specialists for their valuable help by providing information or assisting me in finding it: Members of the Central Texas Astronomical Society, including Johnny Barton, John W. McAnally, and Paul Derrick. Johnny is an officer of the club and has been an active amateur astronomer for more than 20 years. John is also on the staff of the Association of Lunar and Planetary Observers, where he is acting Assistant Coordinator for Transit Timings of the Jupiter Section. Paul is the author of the "Stargazer" column in the *Waco Tribune-Herald*.

Dr. Glenn S. Orton, a Senior Research Scientist at the Jet Propulsion Laboratory of the California Institute of Technology. Glenn is an astronomer and space scientist who specializes in investigating the structure and composition of planetary atmospheres. He is best known for his research on Jupiter and Saturn. I have enjoyed exchanging ideas with Glenn about experiments for modeling astronomy experiments.

Robert Fanick, a chemist at Southwest Research Institute in San Antonio, Texas, and Virginia Malone, a science assessment consultant. These two very special people have provided a great deal of valuable information, which has made this book even more understandable and fun.

A special note of gratitude to these educators who assisted by pretesting the activities and/or by providing scientific information: Holly Harris, China Spring Intermediate, China Spring, Texas; Laura Roberts, St. Matthews Elementary, Louisville, Kentucky; James Roberts, Oldham County High School, Buckner, Kentucky; Anne Skrabanek, homeschooling consultant, Perry, Texas.

Published by John Wiley & Sons, Inc.
Published simultaneously in Canada

Portions of this book have been reprinted from *Janice VanCleave's Animals, Janice VanCleave's Dinosaurs for Every Kid, Janice VanCleave's Earthquakes, Janice VanCleave's Electricity, Janice VanCleave's Geometry for Every Kid, Janice VanCleave's Gravity, Janice VanCleave's Guide to the Best Science Fair Projects, Janice VanCleave's Insects and Spiders, Janice VanCleave's Machines, Janice VanCleave's Magnets, Janice VanCleave's Microscopes and Magnifying Lenses, Janice VanCleave's Molecules, Janice VanCleave's Oceans for Every Kid, Janice VanCleave's Plants, Janice VanCleave's Rocks and Minerals, Janice VanCleave's Solar System, Janice VanCleave's 203 Icy, Freezing, Frosty, Cool, and Wild Experiments, Janice VanCleave's Volcanoes,* and *Janice VanCleave's Weather.*

ISBN: 0-471-32627-5

Printed in the United States of America

10 9 8 7 6 5 4 3

CONTENTS

How to Use This Book

So you're going to do a science fair project. Great! Your work could be chosen as an entry in your school fair and even in regional, state, or national competitions. As a participant in any science fair, you'll get to show off your work and possibly receive achievement awards. But most important, you'll also learn a lot about science by observing and sharing with other fair participants.

A **science project** is like a mystery in which you are the detective searching for answers. Science projects let you practice and exhibit your detective skills. You not only get to select which mystery to solve, but you can creatively design methods for uncovering clues that will lead to the final revelation of who, what, when, where, how, and why. This book will give you guidance and ideas. It's your job to discover the answers!

Solving a scientific mystery, like solving a detective mystery, requires planning and the careful collection of facts. Trying to assemble a project overnight may result in frustration and cheats you out of the fun of being a science detective. With a little planning, though, your science fair experience can be positive and rewarding. This book shows you how to plan ahead. It also gives you the skills and techniques to turn simple experiments into competitive science fair projects. So before you start experimenting, read all of Part I. It explains eight important points you need to know for science fair success. These are the eight points:

1. *The scientific method.* Thinking about solutions to problems and testing each possibility for the best solution is what the scientific method is all about. Chapter 1 describes the steps of the **scientific method** and how all scientists use this basic tool.

2. *Topic research.* Selecting a topic is often considered the hardest part of a science fair project. The research suggestions in Chapter 2 will help make choosing a topic enjoyable. **Research** is the process of collecting information and data. **Data** as used in this book is observations and/or measured facts obtained experimentally. **Topic research** is research used to select a project topic.

3. *Categories.* Chapter 3 provides a list of categories that are used in science fairs. You should identify the category that your project falls into at the beginning of your research. Judges base their evaluation of the content of your project on the category in which you enter it. For example, an A+ botany project incorrectly entered in the math category most likely will receive a lower rating.

4. *Project research.* Once you have selected a topic, it's time to find out as much about it as possible. **Project research** helps you understand a topic. This involves more than just reading materials you find in the library; you'll want to interview people who know a lot about the topic and maybe do exploratory experiments. **Exploratory experiments** as defined in this book are experiments used to gather research. Chapter 4 provides suggestions and directions for doing these. This chapter also gives instructions for requesting printed information from people and organizations.

5. *A sample project.* Chapter 5 guides you step-by-step through the collection of research and its use in identifying a **problem** (a scientific question to be solved), proposing a hypothesis, and designing a project experiment. A **hypothesis** is an idea about the solution to a problem, based on knowledge and research. A **project experiment** is an experiment designed to test a hypothesis. Generally, project experiments are expected to have measurable results. The instructions in this chapter will be invaluable to you as you prepare your own project.

6. *The project report.* A **project report** is the written record of your entire project from start to finish. Chapter 6 shows you how to write a project report after you have completed your project. Your teacher will tell you the level of detail to use in your report. This book gives instructions that can be used for a simple or a complex report.

7. *The display.* Displaying the project can be a fun experience. The examples in Chapter 7 for constructing a backboard should make the experience easy and enjoyable.

8. *Presentation and evaluation.* Chapter 8 helps to prepare you to be judged and tells you what to expect at the fair.

Part II provides project research and ideas for planning and developing projects on 50 science fair topics. These are not intended to be complete projects themselves, but to offer guidelines in developing your own project. The fun of a science fair project lies in exploring a topic in which you're interested, finding and recording information, planning the project experiment, organizing the data, and reaching a conclusion. A science fair project allows you to make your own discoveries. If you have an enthusiastic attitude, you can do it! Let's get started!

I

A GUIDE TO SCIENCE FAIR PROJECTS

Chapter 1

The Scientific Method

A science project is an investigation using the scientific method to discover the answer to a scientific problem. Before starting your project, you need to understand the scientific method. This chapter uses examples to illustrate and explain the basic steps of the scientific method. Chapters 2 through 4 give more details, and Chapter 5 uses the scientific method in a sample project. The **scientific method** is the "tool" that scientists use to find the answers to questions. It is the process of thinking through the possible solutions to a problem and testing each possibility for the best solution. The scientific method involves the following steps: doing research, identifying the problem, stating a hypothesis, conducting project experimentation, and reaching a conclusion.

RESEARCH

Research is the process of collecting information from your own experiences, knowledgeable sources, and data from exploratory experiments. Your first research is used to select a project topic. This is called topic research. For example, you observe a black growth on bread slices and wonder how it got there. Because of this experience, you decide to learn more about mold growth. Your topic will be about fungal reproduction. (**Fungal** refers to plantlike organisms called fungi, which cannot make their own food, and **reproduction** is the making of a new offspring.)

CAUTION: If you are allergic to mold, this is not a topic you would investigate. Choose a topic that is safe for you to do.

Once the topic is selected, you begin what is called project research. This is research to help you understand the topic, express a problem, propose a hypothesis, and design one or more project experiments—experiments designed to test the hypothesis. An example of project research would be to place a fresh loaf of white bread in a bread box and observe the bread over a period of time as an exploratory experiment. The result of this experiment and other research gives you the needed information for the next step—identifying the problem.

Do use many references from printed sources—books, journals, magazines, and newspapers—as well as electronic sources—computer software and on-line services.

Do gather information from professionals—instructors, librarians, and scientists, such as physicians and veterinarians.

Do perform other exploratory experiments, such as those in the 50 science project ideas in Part II.

PROBLEM

The problem is the scientific question to be solved. It is best expressed as an "open-ended" question, which is a question that is answered with a statement, not just a yes or a no. For example, "How does light affect the reproduction of bread mold on white bread?"

Do limit your problem. Note that the previous question is about one life process of molds—reproduction; one type of mold—bread mold; one type of bread—white bread; and one factor that affects its growth—light. To find the answer to a question such as "How does light affect molds?" would require that you test different life processes and an extensive variety of molds.

Do choose a problem that can be solved experimentally. For example, the question "What is a mold?" can be answered by finding the definition of the word *mold* in the dictionary. But, "At room temperature, what is the growth rate of bread mold on white bread?" is a question that can be answered by experimentation.

HYPOTHESIS

A hypothesis is an idea about the solution to a problem, based on knowledge and research. While the hypothesis is a single statement, it is the key to a successful project. All of your project research is done with the goal of expressing a problem, proposing an answer to it—the hypothesis, and designing project experimentation. Then all of your project experimenting will be performed to test the hypothesis. The hypothesis should make a claim about how two factors relate. For example, in the following sample hypothesis, the two relating factors are light and bread mold growth. Here is one example of a hypothesis for the earlier problem question:

"I believe that bread mold does not need light for reproduction on white bread. I base my hypothesis on these facts:

- Organisms with chlorophyll need light to survive. Molds do not have chlorophyll.

- In my exploratory experiment, bread mold grew on white bread kept in a dark bread box."

Do state facts from past experiences or observations on which you based your hypothesis.

Do write down your hypothesis before beginning the project experimentation.

Don't change your hypothesis even if experimentation does not support it. If time permits, repeat or redesign the experiment to confirm your results.

PROJECT EXPERIMENTATION

Project experimentation is the process of testing a hypothesis. The things that have an effect on the experiment are called **variables.** There are three kinds of variables that you need to identify in your experiments: independent, dependent, and controlled. The **independent variable** is the variable you purposely manipulate (change). The **dependent variable** is the variable being observed that changes in response to the independent variable. The variables that are not changed are called **controlled variables.**

The problem in this chapter concerns the effect of light on the reproduction of bread mold. The independent variable for the experiment is light and the dependent variable is bread mold reproduction. A **control** is a test in which the independent variable is kept constant in order to measure changes in the dependent variable. In a control, all variables are identical to the experimental setup—your original setup—except for the independent variable. Factors that are identical in both the experimental setup and the control setup are the controlled variables. For example, prepare the experiment by placing three or four loaves of white bread in cardboard boxes the size of a bread box, one loaf per box. Close the boxes so that they receive no light. If, at the end of a set time period, the mold grows, you might decide that no light was needed for mold reproduction. But, before making this decision, you must determine experimentally if the mold would grow with light. Thus, control groups must be set up of bread that receives light throughout the testing period. Do this by placing an equal number of loaves in comparable-size boxes, but leave them open.

The other variables for the experimental and control setup, such as the environmental conditions for the room where the boxes are placed—temperature and humidity—and the brand of the breads used must be kept the same. These are controlled variables.

Note that when designing the procedure of your project experiment, include steps for measuring the results. For example, to measure the amount of mold growth, you might draw ½ inch (1 cm) squares on a transparent sheet of plastic. This could be placed over the bread and the number of squares with mold growth could be counted. Also, as it is best to perform the experiment more than once, it is also good to have more than one control. You might have one control for every experimental setup.

Do have only one independent variable during an experiment.

Do repeat the experiment more than once to verify your results.

Do have a control.

Do have more than one control, with each being identical.

Do organize data. (See Chapter 5, "A Sample Project," for information on organizing data from experiments.)

PROJECT CONCLUSION

The **project conclusion** is a summary of the results of the project experimentation and a statement of how the results relate to the hypothesis. Reasons for experimental results that are contrary to the hypothesis are included. If applicable, the conclusion can end by giving ideas for further testing.

If your results do not support your hypothesis:

Don't change your hypothesis.

Don't leave out experimental results that do not support your hypothesis.

Do give possible reasons for the difference between your hypothesis and the experimental results.

Do give ways that you can experiment further to confirm the results of your original experiment.

If your results support your hypothesis:

For example, you might say, "As stated in my hypothesis, I believe that light is not necessary for bread mold to reproduce. My experimentation supports the idea that bread mold will reproduce without light. After 21 days, bread mold had grown both on testing samples kept in the dark and also on the control samples in the light. It is possible that temperature is a factor and that the temperature was higher inside the closed boxes due to lack of air circulation. For further testing, I would select temperature as the independent variable and test the effect of temperature changes on the growth of bread mold."

Chapter 2

Topic Research

Now that you understand the scientific method, you are ready to get started.

KEEP A JOURNAL

Purchase a bound notebook to serve as your **journal**. This notebook should contain topic and project research. It should contain not only your original ideas but also ideas you get from printed sources or from people. It should also include descriptions of your exploratory and project experiments as well as diagrams, graphs, and written observations of all your results.

Every entry should be as neat as possible and dated. A neat, orderly journal provides a complete and accurate record of your project from start to finish, and it can be used to write your project report. It is also proof of the time you spent searching out the answers to the scientific mystery you undertook to solve. You will want to display the journal with your completed project.

SELECTING A TOPIC

Obviously you want to get an A+ on your project, win awards at the science fair, and learn many new things about science. Some or all of these goals are possible, but you will have to spend a lot of time working on your project, so choose a topic that interests you. It is best to pick a topic and stick with it, but if you find after some work that your topic is not as interesting as you originally thought, stop and select another one. Since it takes time to develop a good project, it is unwise to

repeatedly jump from one topic to another. You may in fact decide to stick with your original idea even if it is not as exciting as you had expected. You might just uncover some very interesting facts that you didn't know.

Remember that the objective of a science project is to learn more about science. Your project doesn't have to be highly complex to be successful. Excellent projects can be developed that answer very basic and fundamental questions about events or situations encountered on a daily basis. There are many easy ways of selecting a topic. The following are just a few of them.

LOOK CLOSELY AT THE WORLD AROUND YOU

You can turn everyday experiences into a project topic by using the "exploring" question "I wonder . . . ?" For example, you often see cut flowers in a vase of water. These flowers stay pretty for days. If you express this as an exploring question—"I wonder, why do cut flowers last so long in a vase of water?"—you have a good question about plants. But could this be a project topic? Think about it! Is it only the water in the vase that keeps the flowers fresh? Does it matter how the flower stems are cut? By continuing to ask questions, you zero in on the topic of water movement through plants.

Keep your eyes and ears open, and start asking yourself more exploring questions, such as "I wonder, why does my dad paint our house so often?" "I wonder, do different brands of paint last longer?" "I wonder, could I test different kinds of paint on small pieces of wood?" To know more about these things, you can research and design a whole science fair project about the topic of the durability of different kinds of paint. You will be pleasantly surprised at the number of possible project ideas that will come to mind when you begin to look around and use "exploring" questions.

There are an amazing number of comments stated and questions asked by you and those around you each day that could be used to develop science project topics. Be alert and listen for a statement such as "He's a chip off the old block, a southpaw like his dad." If you are in the searching phase of your science fair project, this statement can become an exploring question, such as "I wonder, what percentage of people are left-handed?" or "I wonder, are there more left-handed boys than girls?" These questions could lead you to developing a project about the topic of genetics (inheriting characteristics from one's parents).

CHOOSE A TOPIC FROM YOUR EXPERIENCE

Having a cold is not pleasant, but you could use this "distasteful" experience as a means of selecting a project topic. For example, you may remember that when you had a cold, food did not taste as good. Ask yourself, "I wonder, was this because my nose was stopped up and I couldn't smell the food?" A project about taste and smell could be very successful. After research, you might decide on a problem question such as "How does smell affect taste?" Propose your hypothesis and start designing your project experiment. For more on developing a project, see Chapter 5, "A Sample Project."

FIND A TOPIC IN SCIENCE MAGAZINES

Don't expect topic ideas in science magazines to include detailed instructions on how to perform experiments and design displays.

What you can look for are facts that interest you and that lead you to ask exploring questions. An article about Antarctic animals might bring to mind these exploring questions: "I wonder, how do penguins stay warm?" "I wonder, do fat penguins stay warmer than skinny penguins?" Wow! Body insulation, another great project topic.

SELECT A TOPIC FROM A BOOK ON SCIENCE FAIR PROJECTS OR SCIENCE EXPERIMENTS

Science fair project books, such as this one, can provide you with many different topics to choose from. Even though science experiment books do not give you as much direction as science fair project books, many can provide you with exploratory "cookbook" experiments that tell you what to do, what the results should be, and why. But it will be up to you to provide all the exploring questions and ideas for further experimentation. The 50 project ideas described in this book can further sharpen your skills at expressing exploring questions. A list of different project and experiment books can be found in Appendix A.

SOMETHING TO CONSIDER

You are encouraged not to experiment with vertebrate animals or bacteria. If you do wish to include them in your project, ask your teacher about special permission forms required by your local fair organization. Supervision by a professional, such as a veterinarian or physician, is usually required. The project must cause no harm or undue stress to the subject.

Categories

Every fair has a list of categories, and you need to seek your teacher's advice when deciding which category you should enter your project in. It is important that you enter your project in the correct category. Since science fair judges are required to judge the content of each project based on the category in which it is entered, you would be seriously penalized if you were to enter your project in the wrong category. Listed here are common science fair categories with a brief description of each. Some topics can correctly be placed in more than one category; for example, the structure of plants could be in botany or anatomy. Each of the 50 project ideas in Part II is labeled with the category in which the project could be entered. The categories are

- **astronomy:** The study of the solar system, stars, and the universe.

- **biology:** The study of living things.

  1. **botany:** The study of plants and plant life. Subtopics may include the following:

     a. **anatomy:** The study of the structure of plants, such as cells and seed structure.

     b. **behaviorism:** The study of actions that alter the relationship between a plant and its environment.

     c. **physiology:** The study of life processes of plants, such as propagation, germination, and transportation of nutrients.

  2. **zoology:** The study of animals and animal life. Subtopics may include the following:

     a. **anatomy:** The study of the structure and use of animal body parts, including vision and hearing.

     b. **behaviorism:** The study of actions that alter the relationship between an animal and its environment.

     c. **physiology:** The study of life processes of animals, such as molting, metamorphosis, digestion, reproduction, and circulation.

  3. **ecology:** The study of the relationships of living things to other living things and to their environment.

  4. **microbiology:** The study of microscopic living things or parts of living things.

- **earth science:** The study of the Earth.

  1. **geology:** The study of the Earth, including the composition of its layers, its crust, and its history. Subtopics may include the following:

     a. **fossils:** Remnants or traces of prehistoric life-forms preserved in the Earth's crust.

     b. **mineralogy:** The study of the composition and formation of minerals.

     c. **rocks:** Solids made up of one or more minerals.

    d. seismology: The study of earthquakes.

    e. volcanology: The study of volcanoes.

2. **meteorology:** The study of weather, climate, and the Earth's atmosphere.

3. **oceanography:** The study of the oceans and marine organisms.

4. **paleontology:** The study of prehistoric life-forms.

- **engineering:** The application of scientific knowledge for practical purposes.

- **physical science:** The study of matter and energy.

1. **chemistry:** The study of the materials that substances are made of and how they change and combine.

2. **physics:** The study of forms of energy and the laws of motion. Subtopics include studies in the following areas:

    a. electricity: The form of energy associated with the presence and movement of electric charges.

    b. energy: The capacity to do work.

    c. gravity: The force of attraction between two bodies; the force that pulls objects toward Earth.

    d. machines: Devices that make work easier.

    e. magnetism: The force of attraction or repulsion between magnetic poles, and the attraction that magnets have for magnetic materials.

- **mathematics:** The use of numbers and symbols to study amounts and forms.

    geometry: The branch of mathematics that deals with points, lines, planes, and their relationships to one another.

Chapter 4

Project Research

O nce you have completed the topic research and selected a topic, you are ready to begin your project research. This research is generally more thorough than topic research. Project research is the process of collecting information from knowledgeable sources, such as books, magazines, software, librarians, teachers, parents, scientists, or other professionals. It is also data collected from exploratory experimentation. Read widely on the topic you selected so that you understand it and know about the findings of others. Be sure to give credit where credit is due and record all information and data in your journal.

How successful you are with your project will depend largely on how well you understand your topic. The more you read and question people who know something about your topic, the broader your understanding will be. As a result, it will be easier for you to explain your project to other people, especially a science fair judge. There are two basic kinds of research—primary and secondary.

PRIMARY RESEARCH

Primary research is information you collect on your own. This includes information from exploratory experiments you perform, surveys you take, interviews, and responses to your letters.

Interview people who have special knowledge about your topic. These can include teachers, doctors, scientists, or others whose careers require them to know something related to your topic. Let's say your topic is

about the speed of dinosaurs. "Who would know about dinosaurs?" Start with your science teacher. He or she may have a special interest in dinosaurs or know someone who does. Is there a museum with dinosaur exhibits nearby? Owners of rock and mineral shops may have an interest in fossils and could provide information. Contact the geology department of a local university.

Before contacting the person(s) you want to interview, be prepared. You can do this by making a list of questions that you want to ask. You can even discuss what you know about your topic with someone who knows nothing about it. In so doing, you will be forced to organize your thinking and may even discover additional questions to add to your list. Once your list is complete, you are ready to make your call. Simple rules of courtesy, such as the following, will better ensure that the person called is willing to help.

1. Identify yourself.

2. Identify the school you attend and your teacher.

3. Briefly explain why you are calling. Include information about your project and explain how the person can help you.

4. Request an interview time that is convenient for the person. This could be a telephone or face-to-face interview. Be sure to say that the interview will take about 20 to 30 minutes.

5. Ask if you may tape-record the interview. You can get more information if you are not trying to write down all the answers.

It may be that the person is free when you call, so be prepared to start the interview.

6. Be on time, and be ready to start the interview immediately. Also, be courteous and end the interview on time.

7. Thank the person for the time given and the information provided.

8. A written thank-you note should be sent after the interview, so be sure to record the person's name and address.

You may write letters requesting information instead of interviewing, or write letters in addition to interviewing. Check at the end of articles in periodicals for lists of names and addresses where more information can be obtained. Your librarian can assist you in locating current periodicals related to your topic. If your project deals with a household product, check the packaging for the address of the manufacturer. Send your letter to the public relations department. Ask for all available printed material about your topic. Send your letter as soon as possible to allow time for material to be sent. You can use a form letter similar to the one shown here to make it easier to send it to as many different people and organizations as you can find.

Lacey Russell
231 Kids Lane
Woodlands, OK 74443

August 31, 2005

The Dial Corporation
15101 North Scottsdale Road
Station 5028
Scottsdale, AZ 85254

Dear Director:

I am a sixth-grade student currently working on a science project for the Davin Elementary Science Fair. My project is about conditions affecting bacterial growth. I would greatly appreciate any information you could send me on the "anti-bacterial" properties of your product. Please send the information as soon as possible.

Thank you very much.

Sincerely,

Lacey Russell

SECONDARY RESEARCH

Secondary research is information and/or data that someone else has collected. You find this type of information in written sources (books, magazines, and newspapers) and in electronic sources (CD-ROM encyclopedias, software packages, or on-line services, such as the Internet). When you use a secondary source, be sure to note where you got the information for future reference. If you are required to write a report, you will need the following information for a bibliography or to give credit for any quotes or illustrations you use.

Book

Author's name, title of book, place of publication, publisher, copyright date, and pages read or quoted.

Magazine or periodical

Author's name, title of article, title of magazine, volume and issue number and date of publication, and page numbers of article.

Newspaper

Author's name, title of article, name of newspaper, date of publication, and section and page numbers.

Encyclopedia

Name of encyclopedia, volume number, title of article, place of publication, publisher, year of publication, and page numbers of article.

CD-ROM encyclopedia or software package

Name of program, version or release number, name of supplier, and place where supplier is located.

Documents from on-line services

Author of document (if known), title of document, name of organization that posted document, place where organization is located, date given on document, on-line address or mailing address where document is available.

USE YOUR RESEARCH

Now you are ready to use the project research information and data collected to express the problem, propose a hypothesis, and design and perform one or more project experiments. The project research will also be useful in writing the project report. The following chapters, 5 through 8, guide you step-by-step through a sample project from start to finish. You may want to read these chapters more than once and refer back to them as you progress through your project.

Chapter 5

A Sample Project

Pick a topic. Each of the 50 project ideas in Part II begins with a detailed exploratory experiment. Read some or all of these easy experiments to discover the topic you like best and want to know more about. Regardless of the topic you choose for the science fair, what you discover from any of these experiments will make you more knowledgeable about science.

How can you turn a project idea from this book into your own unique project?

This chapter uses a project idea similar in format to those found in Part II. The detailed exploratory experiment will be referred to as the sample experiment and is used for several purposes. Like all exploratory experiments, its main purpose is to provide research data on which to base a hypothesis. But in this chapter, it is also used as a model for a project experiment. During the experimentation phase of your project, you can use the following data-collecting techniques and other ideas to design, develop, and fine-tune your project.

KEEPING YOUR PROJECT JOURNAL

Every step of the way, you will keep a journal in which to record the progress of the project. After experimentation has been completed, the journal will be very useful to you when you begin to write your project report. Chapter 6 explains how to write a project report.

TITLE AND PROBLEM QUESTION

The title and problem question for the sample experiment (see Figure 5.1) may or may

How High?

PROBLEM

When is the Sun at its highest altitude during the day?

Figure 5.1 Sample Experiment Title and Problem

Materials

pencil

5 tablespoons (75 ml) plaster of paris

2 tablespoons (30 ml) tap water

3-ounce (90-ml) paper cup

masking tape

36-inch (1-meter) piece of string

yardstick (meterstick)

protractor

helper

Figure 5.2 Sample Experiment Materials List

not be acceptable for your project. Because you'll know so much more after doing the sample experiment and other research, let's wait before deciding on the title and problem question.

MATERIALS

As Figure 5.2 shows, all the materials for the sample experiment, like those for all the experiments in this book, can be found around the house or purchased without much money at a local grocery or hardware store. Collect the supplies before you start the experiment. You will have less frustration and more fun if all the materials are ready before you start. Substituting materials is not suggested, but if something is not available, ask an adult's advice before using different materials.

Note that each of the project ideas in Part II contains more than one exploratory experiment. The "Materials" section at the beginning of each project contains only the materials for the first experiment. Be sure to read through the entire project prior to starting to determine all the materials you'll need to complete each experiment. *NOTE: Approximate metric equivalents have been given after all English measurements. Both English and metric units are given in this book, but the metric system is often suggested for science fair projects because of its ease in measuring small quantities.*

PROCEDURE

The "Procedure" section for the sample experiment (see Figure 5.3) contains the steps needed to complete the experiment. Figure 5.4 shows the procedure setup. As described in Chapter 1, a variable is anything that has an effect on the experiment. In the sample experiment, the Sun's altitude is mea-

Figure 5.4   Procedure Setup

sured at specific times during the day. The time of day is the independent, or manipulated, variable. The measured altitude of the Sun at this time is the dependent, or responding, variable. All other variables, such as the latitude and season, are the controlled, or constant, variables.

RESULTS

Before you can state the results of an experiment, you must first organize all the data collected during experimentation. Numbers, called "raw data," have little meaning unless you organize and label them. Data from each experiment needs to be written down in an orderly way in your journal. Use a **table** (a diagram that uses words and numbers in columns and rows to represent data) to record data (see Figure 5.5). Use a graph, such as a **bar graph** (a diagram that uses

---

Procedure

CAUTION: Do not look directly at the Sun. It can damage your eyes.

1. Use the pencil point to mix the plaster of paris and water in the paper cup. Stand the pencil, eraser end up, vertically in the mixture and do not disturb until the mixture hardens. This may take 30 minutes or more. *NOTE: Do not wash plaster down the drain. It can clog the drain.*

2. Tear away the paper cup above the hardened plaster and tape one end of the string to the top of the pencil.

3. Starting at the 0 end of the measuring stick, tape the protractor so that it stands perpendicular to the surface of the measuring stick with the 0 degree mark on the protractor even with the surface of the stick. The end of the stick opposite the protractor will be called the pointer end.

4. Place a piece of tape across the measuring stick even with the center of the protractor. Make a mark across the tape to mark the center of the protractor. This will be called the measuring line.

5. At 8:00 A.M. standard time, set the measuring stick on a flat surface outdoors in a sunny area with its pointer end toward the Sun.

6. Set the cup in the middle of the stick. Adjust the pointer end of the stick so that the shadow cast by the pencil falls on the stick. Move the cup back and forth along the stick until the end of the pencil's shadow touches the measuring line.

7. Hold the cup in place and extend the string between the top of the pencil and the measuring line. Ask a helper to read the angle where the string crosses the protractor.

8. Repeat steps 5 through 7 at these times during the day: 10:00 A.M., 12:00 P.M. (noon), 2:00 P.M., and 4:00 P.M.

NOTE: If the shadow is longer than the measuring stick, place two measuring sticks end to end.

Figure 5.3   Sample Experiment Procedure

SUN ALTITUDE	
Time	**Altitude (degrees, °)**
8:00 A.M.	14
10:00 A.M.	28
12:00 P.M.	42
2:00 P.M.	28
4:00 P.M.	14

Figure 5.5   Example of a Table for Sample Experiment

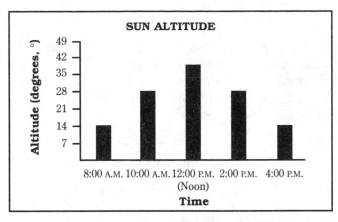

Figure 5.6   Example of a Bar Graph

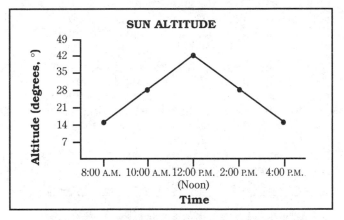

Figure 5.7   Example of a Line Graph

bars to represent data) similar to the one shown in Figure 5.6 to **analyze** (separate and examine) data. Figure 5.7 shows another way to represent the data. This figure is a **line graph** (a diagram that uses lines to express patterns of change).

There are other useful ways to represent data. A circle graph, or **pie chart,** is a **chart** (data or other information in the form of a table, graph, or list) that shows information in percentages. The larger the section of the circle, the greater the percentage represented. The whole circle represents 100 percent, or the total amount. For example, a pie chart can be used to represent the results of an experiment determining the direction of the Sun at different times during one day, from sunrise to sunset. To make a pie chart, first record the directions at different times in a table, as

SUN DIRECTION

Time	Direction
6:00 A.M. (sunrise)	east (E)
8:00 A.M.	southeast (SE)
10:00 A.M.	southeast (SE)
12:00 P.M. (noon)	south (S)
2:00 P.M.	southwest (SW)
4:00 P.M.	southwest (SW)
6:00 P.M. (sunset)	west (W)

Figure 5.8   Table of Sun Directions

shown in Figure 5.8. Prepare a second table expressing the number of hours the Sun is in the eastern (E and SE) and western (W and SW) parts of the sky, as shown in Figure 5.9. Then, express the same data as percentages in a pie chart, as shown in Figure 5.10. Note that illustrations of rising and setting suns are placed around the circle to add interest to the data displayed.

A pictograph could be used to represent the results of an experiment measuring the Sun's altitude at noon over a three-month period. A **pictograph** is a chart that contains symbols representing data, such as quantities of an object. In the pictograph shown in Figure 5.11, each sun represents an altitude of 4 degrees. Pictographs are easy to read and can add a little fun to your data display.

The data charted in Figure 5.5 was used to write a statement of the changes in altitude of the Sun as observed in the sample project, as shown in Figure 5.12.

Photographs are another way to display data. Have someone take a photograph of you performing the experiment, as in Figure 5.4,

SUN DIRECTION

Direction	Hours	Percentage of Day
eastern (E and SE)	6	50
western (W and SW)	6	50

Figure 5.9   Table of Sun Directions

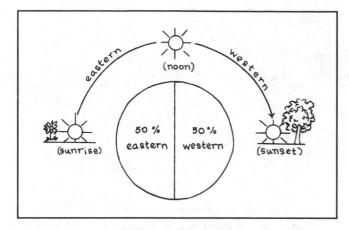

Figure 5.10 Pie Chart of Sun Directions

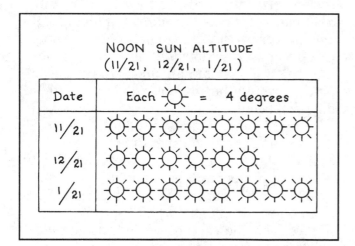

Figure 5.11 Example of a Pictograph

Results

The altitude of the Sun increases before noon, is highest at noon, then decreases after noon.

Figure 5.12 Sample Experiment Results

or take photos of the procedure setup to use as part of the project display. Use the format of the procedure shown in Figure 5.3 as a guideline to design your own project experiment.

WHY?

Figure 5.13 shows an explanation of the results of the sample experiment. This information, along with the other research, will be used to develop a project problem, hypothesis, and experiment(s).

Why?

Extending the line formed by the string points to the position of the Sun. The angle between this line and the measuring stick is equal to the angle of the Sun above the horizon. Thus, the angle measured is equal to the Sun's **altitude** (angular height above the horizon). At noon, standard time, the Sun is at or near its highest altitude during the day.

The Sun appears to move across the sky. Actually, the Sun is not moving. Instead, the Earth is rotating on its axis, giving the illusion that the Sun is moving across the sky. Since the axis of the Earth is tilted in relationship to the Sun, the maximum height of the Sun in the sky during the day changes as the Earth **revolves** (moves in a curved path about an object) around the Sun.

Figure 5.13 Sample Experiment Explanation

LET'S EXPLORE

This is the point at which you begin to ask different exploring questions as the basis for more research ideas, such as "I wonder, where on Earth does the Sun reach its highest altitude?" or "I wonder, how does the latitude of a location affect the Sun's altitude? Wow! That last question is great." You'll find that the more you think about the sample experiment, the more exploring questions you'll be able to think of and the better your questions will be. Figure 5.14 shows exploring questions and how to find their answers by changing the sample experiment. The experiments in this and the following sections could be performed and the data added to the research information. Another use would be as aids in designing your project experiment(s). Before any further experimentation, read through "Let's Explore," "Show Time!", and "Check It Out!".

LET'S EXPLORE

1. Does the Sun's maximum altitude change from day to day? Repeat the experiment measuring the Sun's altitude at noon for 7 or more days.

2. How does the Sun's maximum altitude compare at different latitudes on the same day? Ask friends at latitudes higher and lower than yours to perform the original experiment at noon on a specific day. Compare and report the results.

Figure 5.14   Sample Experiment "Let's Explore"

SHOW TIME!

The "Show Time!" section in Figure 5.15 shows two ideas related to the sample experiment. It offers different experimental ideas for further investigation of the topic, as well as more ideas for designing your own experi-ments. (When you design your own experi-ments, make sure to get an adult's approval if you use supplies or procedures other than those given in this book.) Again, these experi-ments can provide project research or ideas for designing your project experiment(s).

CHECK IT OUT!

At this point, you are ready for in-depth research on the topic. The questions asked at this point (see Figure 5.16) require some sec-ondary research. A good place to start your research is the library. Earth science books have sections on the Sun, its motion, its loca-tion, and the heat from its rays. Science exper-iment books are also a good source of information and provide experiments to use as well.

You will discover from these sources that as the Earth revolves around the Sun, the Sun's maximum altitude during the day increases and decreases. The higher the Sun's altitude, the more direct the rays and generally the higher the temperature. Wow!

SHOW TIME!

1a. As Earth revolves around the Sun, its axis always points in the same direction. But since Earth's axis is tilted 23.5 degrees in relation-ship to its orbit, the ends of the axis tilt toward the Sun during part of the year and away from the Sun for part of the year. As a result, the altitude of the Sun changes during the year. These changes produce **seasons** (periods of the year characterized by specific weather). The four seasons on Earth are spring, summer, fall and winter. Demonstrate the position of Earth in its orbit when the Sun is at its highest altitude in the Northern Hemisphere. This would be summer, the warmest season. Prepare an Earth model by using a rounded toothpick to draw a circle around the middle of a grape-size ball of modeling clay. Insert the toothpick through the clay ball so that the line you just drew circles the clay as the Earth's equator circles the globe. Use another grape-size piece of clay to support the model. With a drawing compass, draw a 1-inch (2.5-cm) circle in the center of a 12-by-12-inch (30-by-30-cm) piece of white poster board. Label the circle "Sun." On the edges of the poster board, label these seasons in a counterclockwise order: "Spring," "Summer," "Fall," "Winter." Stand the Earth model on the edge of the poster board labeled "Summer" with the top of the toothpick tilted toward the Sun and the wall beyond Sun. Note that the top part of the model (the Northern Hemisphere) tilts toward the Sun and the bot-tom part (the Southern hemisphere) tilts away from the Sun.

1b. With the toothpick still tilted toward the wall, move the model in a counterclockwise direc-tion from one season to the next. Prepare a diagram indicating the areas of Earth where the Sun is at its highest altitude during each season.

Figure 5.15   Sample Experiment "Show Time!"

That's why it's so hot during the summer when the Sun is so high in the sky. This is a real-life experience that you are using to help you with your project. You will want to draw from your personal experiences, not only when looking for a topic as discussed in Chapter 2, but also during your project research.

CHECK IT OUT!

1. In the Northern Hemisphere, the Sun is at its highest altitude on or about June 21. This time is called the *summer solstice*. At this time, the apparent motion of the Sun reaches its northernmost point, which is the *Tropic of Cancer* (latitude 23.5 degrees north of the equator). Find out more about the apparent motion of the Sun. Where is its southernmost point and when does it reach this point? What and when is the winter solstice? What and when are the equinoxes?

2. Earth's equator receives about 2½ times as much heat during the year as does the areas around its Poles. How does the angle of the Sun's rays affect the heating of Earth's surface?

Figure 5.16   Sample Experiment "Check It Out!"

PROBLEM AND HYPOTHESIS

After collecting and analyzing your project research, it's time to zero in on the problem. Let's say you've decided to investigate the relationship between the angle of the Sun's noon rays and air temperature. The question doesn't have to be complex and wordy to be good. Make it as simple and to the point as possible. Look at these two examples:

1. How does the angle of the Sun's rays at noon affect seasonal temperatures?

2. Does the difference in the angle of the Sun's rays at noon affect the amount of energy received by Earth's surface? If so, how does that difference affect temperature during different seasons?

Both of the examples have the same goal of discovering how the angle of the Sun's rays affects air temperature, but the first example is short and quickly read. Keep in mind that your project will be judged at the science fair, and you want each judge to know immediately the single purpose for your project.

With your problem stated, it's time to develop the hypothesis. The hypothesis might be "I believe that the size of Sun ray angles at noon cause seasonal temperatures, small angles causing warm temperatures and large angles causing cold temperatures." This hypothesis is based on these facts:

- In my research, I discovered that shadow angles are the same as the angles of the Sun's rays, and the shadow angles change during the day as well as from season to season.

- In my exploratory experiment, shadow angles were least at or near noon and greatest in early morning and late evening.

- I've observed that early morning and late evening are generally the coolest parts of a day and midday is warmest.

NOW YOU'RE ON YOUR OWN

Test your hypothesis by designing a project experiment(s) to determine if the angle of the Sun's rays during different seasons affects temperature. You might use the instrument in the exploratory experiment to measure the Sun's ray angle. The ray angle would be equal to the angle of the pencil's shadow, which is the angle between the top of the pencil and the stretched string. Since the least shadow angle is at or near noon, a comparison of shadow angles and temperatures at noon during different seasons can be made. Once you have designed one or more experiments, collect data, construct tables and graphs, draw diagrams, and take photos to represent results. The control can be when the Sun is at its lowest or highest angle.

UNEXPECTED RESULTS?

What do you do if your results are not what you expected? First, if there is time, repeat the experiment and make sure everything is done properly. If there isn't time for this, or if you get the same unexpected results again, *don't panic.* A scientist's hypothesis often is not supported by his or her experiments. Report the truth in your conclusion. Assuming your research supported your hypothesis, state your hypothesis as before, but truthfully say that while your research backed up your hypothesis, your experimental results did not. Say what you expected and what actually happened. Report everything—if anything supported the hypothesis, identify it. Continue by giving reasons why you think the results did not support your original ideas. Make your explanation scientific. For example, if you think the experimental materials might have been moved during the experiment:

Do say: "There is a possibility that I did not consider daylight savings time each time I took measurements. This problem could be solved by always using the same watch or clock set to standard time."

Don't say: "My sister gave me the wrong time. I need to find someone who is better at telling time."

It may be that after evaluating your data, you may decide that your original hypothesis was incorrect. If so, say this and give reasons for your change of mind.

Now it's time to sum up the entire project by writing a detailed report. Review the next chapter for advice on how to put together a science-fair project report.

Chapter 6

The Project Report

Your report is the written record of your entire project from start to finish. When read by a person unfamiliar with your project, the report should be clear and detailed enough for the reader to know exactly what you did, why you did it, what the results were, whether or not the experimental evidence supported your hypothesis, and where you got your research information. This written document is your spokesperson when you are not present to explain your project, but more than that, it documents all your work.

Much of the report will be copied from your journal. By recording everything in your journal as the project progresses, all you need to do in preparing the report is to organize and neatly copy the journal's contents. Tables, graphs, and diagrams can be neatly and colorfully prepared. If possible, use a computer to prepare some or all of these data displays.

Check with your teacher for the order and content of the report as regulated by the local fair. Generally, a project report should be typewritten, double-spaced, and bound in a folder or notebook. It should contain a title page, a table of contents, an abstract, an introduction, the experiment(s) and data, a conclusion, a list of sources, and acknowledgments. The rest of this chapter describes these parts of a project report and gives examples based on the sample project in Chapter 5.

TITLE PAGE

The content of the title page varies. Some fairs require that only the title of the project be centered on the page. Normally, your name would not appear on this page during judging.

Your teacher can give you the local fair's rules for this. The title should be attention getting. It should capture the theme of the project but should not be the same as the problem question. A good title for the sample project detailed in Chapter 5 is shown in Figure 6.1.

Up and Down:
Seasonal Temperature versus Sun Ray Angle

Figure 6.1   A Project Title

TABLE OF CONTENTS

The second page of your report is the table of contents. It should contain a list of everything in the report that follows the contents page, as shown in Figure 6.2

Contents

1. Abstract
2. Introduction
3. Experiment(s)
4. Data
5. Conclusion
6. Sources
7. Acknowledgments

Figure 6.2   A Table of Contents

ABSTRACT

The abstract is a brief overview of the project. It should not be more than 1 page and should include the project title, a statement of the purpose, a hypothesis, a brief description of the procedure, and the results. There is no one way to write an abstract, but it should be brief, as shown in Figure 6.3. Often, a copy of the abstract must be submitted to the science fair officials on the day of judging, and it is a good idea to have copies available at your display. This gives judges something to refer to when making final decisions. It might also be used to prepare an introduction by a special award sponsor, so do a thorough job on this part of your report.

Abstract
Up and Down:
Seasonal Temperature versus Sun Ray Angle

The purpose of this project was to find out whether the angle of the Sun's rays at noon affects seasonal temperatures. The experiments involved measuring the air temperature and the angle of the Sun's rays at noon during different seasons. This was done by recording air temperature and measuring the angle of shadows at noon on the first day of the month from October through April.

The measurements confirmed my hypothesis that as the angle of the Sun's rays decreases during the year, the outdoor temperature increases. These findings led me to believe that seasonal temperatures are the result of the difference in the angle of the Sun's rays. As the ray angle decreases, sunlight is more concentrated on an area, resulting in a higher temperature.

I discovered that during seasons with high temperatures, the angle of the Sun's rays is lower than during seasons with low temperatures.

Figure 6.3   An Abstract

INTRODUCTION

The introduction is a statement of your purpose, along with background information that led you to make this study. It should contain a brief statement of your hypothesis based on your research. In other words, it should state what information or knowledge you had that led you to hypothesize the answer to the project's problem question. Make references to information or experiences that led you to choose the project's purpose. If your teacher requires footnotes, then include one for each information source

you have used. The introduction shown in Figure 6.4 does not use footnotes.

Introduction

The air temperature generally changes quite a bit during the day, but any change from one day to the next at the same time of day is, as a rule, relatively small. But the temperature of some regions changes significantly over the course of a year, resulting in different seasons.

While reading about my project topic, the effect of the angle of the Sun's rays at noon on seasonal temperatures, I thought about my own experience of the Sun's high noon altitude and small shadow angles occurring at the same time as high summer temperatures. Further research provided the facts that as the angle of the Sun's rays decreases, the more concentrated the rays, thus the hotter the area of Earth receiving them. I reasoned that the angle of the Sun's rays at noon must change during the year.

My curiosity about the relation of angle of the Sun's rays to temperature resulted in a project that has as its purpose to discover how the angle of the Sun's rays affects air temperature during the year and thus causes seasons. Based on previous stated research and the fact that it is cooler in the morning when the angle of the Sun's rays is least due to the Sun's low altitude, my hypothesis was that as the angle of the Sun's rays increases during the year, the outdoor temperature increases, causing seasons.

Figure 6.4   Introduction

EXPERIMENTS

Each project experiment should be listed in the experiment section of the report. Experiments should include the problem of the experiment, followed first by a list of the materials used and the amount of each, then by the procedural steps in outline or paragraph form, as shown in Figure 6.5. Note that the experiment described in Figure 6.5 determines the average monthly angle of the Sun's noon rays during 7 consecutive months. A second experiment is needed to measure the average temperature of each month. The experiments should be written so that anyone could follow them and expect to get the same results.

Experiment

Purpose

To determine the angle of the Sun's rays at noon (standard time) during different seasons.

Materials

yardstick (meterstick)

cup with pencil and string prepared in the Sample Experiment

protractor

Procedure

1. At around 11:45 A.M., set the measuring stick on a flat surface in a sunny area outdoors with its pointer end facing the horizon directly below the Sun.
2. Set the cup in the middle of the stick. Move the pointer end of the stick so that the shadow cast by the pencil falls on the stick.
3. At 12:00 P.M. (noon), move the cup back and forth along the stick until the end of the shadow touches the measuring line. *NOTE: If the shadow is longer than the measuring stick, place two measuring sticks end to end.*
4. Hold the cup in place and extend the string from the top of the pencil to the measuring line. Ask a helper to use the protractor to measure the angle between the pencil and string.
5. Repeat steps 1 through 3 one or more times each week during 6 or more consecutive months.
6. Average the angles measured for each month.

Figure 6.5   An Experiment

SUN RAY ANGLES AT NOON

Month	Average Monthly Angle (degrees, °)
October	40
November	31
December	24
January	31
February	40
March	48
April	56

Figure 6.6   A Table

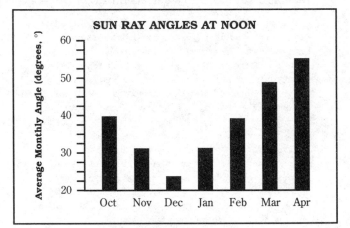

Figure 6.7   Example of a Bar Graph

DATA

Following each experiment, include all measurements and observations that you took during each experiment. Graphs, tables, and charts created from your data should be labeled and, if possible, colorful. Figure 6.6 shows a table and Figure 6.7 a bar graph for the experiment shown in Figure 6.5. If there is a large amount of data, you may choose to put most of it in an appendix, which can be placed in a separate binder or notebook. If you do separate the material, a summary of the data should be placed in the data section of the report.

CONCLUSION

The conclusion summarizes, in about one page or less, what you discovered based on your experimental results, as shown in Figure 6.8. The conclusion states the hypothesis and indicates whether the data supports it. The conclusion can also include a brief description of plans for exploring ideas for future experiments.

SOURCES

Sources are the places where you obtained information, including all of the written materials as well as the people you have interviewed. For the written materials, write a bibliography. See "Secondary Research" in Chapter 4 for information about bibliographies. People that you interviewed should be listed separately, in alphabetical order by last name. Provide title and with permission give their address and business phone number, as shown in Figure 6.9. Do not list home addresses or phone numbers.

Conclusion

As stated in my hypothesis, I believe that the size of Sun ray angles at noon cause seasonal temperatures, small angles causing warm temperatures and large angles causing cold temperatures. The experimental data supported my hypothesis, indicating a direct relation between the angle of the Sun's rays and the air temperature. This direct relation between the ray angles and the temperatures was found to apply over different seasons. The smaller the ray angle, the warmer the season, and the greater the angle, the cooler the season. Experimental data also showed an inverse relation between the Sun's noon altitude and the angle of the Sun's rays; thus, as the altitude of the Sun increases, its ray angle decreases. The experiments confirmed that more direct Sun rays (those with the least angle) heat the earth more.

Through my research as well as experience, I discovered that the length of each day is not exactly the same. Ideas for a future experiment would be to determine the effect of day length on the average daily temperature.

Figure 6.8   A Project Conclusion

Source Interviewed

Lynn, Jennifer
Astronomer
100 Rainy Drive
San Francisco, California 00001
(001) 222-0000

Figure 6.9   An Interview Source

ACKNOWLEDGMENTS

Even though technically your project is to be your work alone, it is permissible to have some help. The acknowledgments is not a list of names, but a short paragraph stating the names of the people and how they helped you, as shown in Figure 6.10. Note that when listing family members or relatives, it is generally not necessary to include their names.

Acknowledgments

I would like to thank the members of my family who assisted me with this project; my mother, who proofread and typed my report, and my father and sister, who assisted in the construction of the display board.

A special note of thanks to Dr. Lauren Russell, professor of astronomy at Lacey University, and to Davin Wade, her assistant, for their expert guidance.

Figure 6.10   Acknowledgments

Chapter 7

The Display

Your science fair display represents all the work that you have done. It should consist of a backboard, the project report, and anything that represents your project, such as models made, items studied, photographs, surveys, and the like. It must tell the story of the project in such a way that it attracts and holds the interest of the viewer. It has to be thorough, but not too crowded, so keep it simple.

The allowable size and shape of the display backboard can vary, so you will have to check the rules for your science fair. Most exhibits are allowed to be 48 inches (122 cm) wide, 30 inches (76 cm) deep, and 108 inches (274 cm) high (including the table it stands on). These are maximum measurements, so your display may be smaller than this. A three-sided backboard is usually the best way to display your work. Sturdy cardboard or other heavy material is easier to work with and is less likely to be damaged during transportation to the fair. Wooden panels can be cut and hinged together. Some office supply stores sell inexpensive premade backboards. If these are not available in your area, see Appendix C for science supply companies from which you can order inexpensive premade backboards.

Purchased backboards generally come in two colors, black and white. You can use a different color by covering the backboard with self-stick colored shelving paper or cloth. For items placed on the backboard, select colors that stand out but don't distract a viewer from the material being presented. For example, if everything is in

fluorescent colors, the bright colors will be what catches the eye instead of your work.

The title and other headings should be neat and large enough to be read at a distance of about 3 feet (1 m). A short title is often eye-catching. Self-sticking letters, of various sizes and colors, for the title and headings can be purchased at office supply stores and stuck to the backboard. You can cut your own letters out of construction paper or stencil the letters for all the titles directly onto the backboard. You can also use a word processor to print the title and other headings.

Some teachers have set rules about the position of the information on the backboard. The following headings are examples: Problem, Hypothesis, Experiment (materials and procedure), Data, Results, Conclusion, and Next

Figure 7.1   Example of a Good Display

Time. The project title should go at the top of the center panel, and the remaining material needs to be placed neatly in some order. Figure 7.1 shows one way of placing the material. The heading "Next Time," though not always required, may be included if desired. It would follow the conclusion and contain a brief description of plans for future development of the project. This information could be included in the conclusion rather than under a separate heading.

You want a display that the judges will remember positively. So before you glue everything down, lay the board on a flat surface and arrange the materials a few different ways. This will help you decide on the most suitable and attractive presentation. Figure 7.1 shows what a good display might look like.

HELPFUL HINTS

1. Place all typed material on a colored backing, such as construction paper. Leave a border of about ¼ to ½ inch (0.63 to 1.25 cm) around the edges of each piece of typed material. Use a paper cutter so that the edges will be straight.

2. Make the project title stand out by using larger letters for it and smaller letters for the headings.

3. To arrange the letters on the backboard, first lay the letters out on the board without attaching them. Then, use a yardstick (meterstick) and pencil to draw a straight, light guideline where the bottom of each letter should line up. This will help you keep the lettering straight. Before adhering everything, ask the opinion of other students, teachers, or family members.

4. If you need electricity for your project, be sure the wiring meets all safety standards.

5. Bring an emergency kit with extra letters, glue, tape, construction paper the color of the backboard, stapler, scissors, pencils, pens, touch-up paint, markers, and so forth. This kit should contain anything that you think you might need to make last-minute repairs to the display.

6. Before standing your backboard on the display table, cover the table with a colored cloth. Choose a color that matches the color scheme of the backboard. This will help to separate your project from other projects displayed on either side.

DO'S AND DON'TS

Do use computer-generated graphs.

Do display photos representing the procedure and the results.

Do use contrasting colors.

Do limit the number of colors used.

Do display models when applicable. If possible, make the models match the color scheme of the backboard.

Do attach charts neatly. If there are many, place them on top of each other so that the top chart can be lifted to reveal the ones below.

Do balance the arrangement of materials on the backboard. This means to evenly distribute the materials on the board so that they cover about the same amount of space on each panel.

Do use rubber cement or double-sided tape to attach papers. White school glue causes the paper to wrinkle.

Don't leave large empty spaces on the backboard.

Don't leave the table in front of the backboard empty. Display your models (if any), report, copies of your abstract, and your journal here.

Don't hang electrical equipment on the backboard so that the electric cord runs down the front of the backboard.

Don't make the title or headings hard to read by using uneven lettering, words with letters of different colors, or disorganized placement of materials.

Don't hand-print the letters on the backboard.

Don't attach folders that fall open on the backboard.

Don't make mistakes in spelling words or writing formulas.

Figure 7.2 shows how *not* to set up your display.

Figure 7.2   Example of a Bad Display

SAFETY

Anything that is or could be hazardous to other students or the public is *prohibited* and cannot be displayed. The following is a list of things that are generally unacceptable for display. Your teacher has access to a complete list of safety rules from your local science fair officials. Your project topic should be approved by your teacher before beginning. This prevents you from working on an unsafe project and from wasting time on a project that would be disqualified. Models or photographs can be used instead of things that are restricted from display.

Unacceptable for Display

1. Live animals
2. Microbial cultures or fungi, living or dead
3. Animal or human parts, except for teeth, hair, nails, and dried animal bones
4. Liquids, including water
5. Chemicals and/or their empty containers, including caustics, acids, and household cleaners
6. Open or concealed flames
7. Batteries with open-top cells
8. Combustible materials
9. Aerosol cans of household solvents
10. Controlled substances, poisons, or drugs
11. Any equipment or device that would be hazardous to the public
12. Sharp items, such as syringes, knives, and needles
13. Gases

Chapter 8

Presentation and Evaluation

Your teacher may require that you give an oral presentation of your project for your class. Make it short but complete. Presenting in front of your classmates may be the hardest part of the project. You want to do your best, so prepare and practice, practice, practice. If possible, tape your practice presentation on a tape recorder or have someone videotape you. Review the tape and/or video and evaluate yourself. Review your notes and practice again.

Practicing an oral presentation will also be helpful for the science fair itself. The judges give points for how clearly you are able to discuss the project and explain its purpose, procedure, results, and conclusion. The display should be organized so that it explains everything, but your ability to discuss your project and answer the questions of the judges convinces them that you did the work and understand what you have done. Practice a speech in front of friends, and invite them to ask questions. If you do not know the answer to a question, never guess or make up an answer or just say "I don't know." Instead, say that you did not discover that answer during your research, and then offer other information that you found of interest about the project. Be proud of the project, and approach the judges with enthusiasm about your work.

You can decide on how best to dress for a class presentation, but for the local fair, it is wise to make a special effort to look nice. You are representing your work. In effect, you are acting as a salesperson for your project, and you want to present the very best image possible. Your appearance shows how much personal pride you have in yourself, and that is the first step in introducing your product, your science project.

JUDGING INFORMATION

Most fairs have similar point systems for judging a science fair project, but you may be better prepared by understanding that judges generally start by thinking that each student's project is average. Then, he or she adds or subtracts points from that. A student should receive more points for accomplishing the following:

1. Project Objectives

   - Presenting original ideas
   - Stating the problem clearly
   - Defining the variables and using controls
   - Relating background reading to the problem

2. Project Skills

   - Being knowledgeable about equipment used
   - Performing the experiments with little or no assistance except as required for safety
   - Demonstrating the skills required to do all the work necessary to obtain the data reported

3. Data Collection

   - Using a journal to collect data and research

- Repeating the experiment to verify the results
- Spending an appropriate amount of time to complete the project
- Having measurable results

4. Data Interpretation
- Using tables, graphs, and illustrations in interpreting data
- Using research to interpret data collected
- Collecting enough data to make a conclusion
- Using only data collected to make a conclusion

5. Project Presentation (Written Materials/ Interview/Display)
- Having a complete and comprehensive report
- Answering questions accurately
- Using the display during oral presentation
- Justifying conclusions on the basis of experimental data
- Summarizing what was learned
- Presenting a display that shows creative ability and originality
- Presenting an attractive and interesting display

DO'S AND DON'TS AT THE FAIR

Do bring activities, such as puzzles to work on or a book to read, to keep yourself occupied at your booth. There may be a lengthy wait before the first judge arrives, and even between judges.

Do become acquainted with your neighboring presenters. Be friendly and courteous.

Do ask neighboring presenters about their projects, and tell them about yours if they express interest. These conversations pass time and help relieve nervous tension that can build when you are waiting to be evaluated. You may also discover techniques for research that you can use for next year's project.

Do have fun.

Don't laugh or talk loud. This may affect the person nearby who is being judged.

Don't forget that you are an ambassador for your school. This means that your attitude and behavior influence how people at the fair think about you and the other students at your school.

50 SCIENCE FAIR PROJECT IDEAS

Astronomy

Brighter

PROBLEM

Why are planets so bright in the sky?

Materials

transparent tape
sheet of office paper
sheet of 9-by-12-inch (22.5-by-30-cm) white
    construction paper
medium-size box with one side at least
    9-by-12-inches (22.5 × 30 cm)
yardstick (meterstick)
3 to 4 books
flashlight

Procedure

1. Tape the office paper to a wall so that its bottom edge rests on the floor. This paper represents the screen in a **photometer** (an instrument that measures the brightness of light) located at a point on the Earth.

2. Tape the white construction paper to one side of the box. This paper represents the surface or **atmosphere** (layer of gas surrounding a celestial body) of a planet.

3. Stand the box 12 inches (30 cm) from the screen, with the paper-covered side of the box facing the screen.

4. Use the books to raise the flashlight so that it is at an angle to the paper on the box and its light shines on the center of the construction paper.

5. Turn the flashlight on, then darken the room. Observe the brightness of the photometer screen.

6. Turn the flashlight off and again observe the brightness of the screen.

Results

The screen brightens when the flashlight is on.

Why?

The Sun and other stars are **luminous** (giving off light). But the Moon and planets, even though they shine, are not luminous. These **celestial bodies** (natural objects in the sky, such as stars, suns, moons, and planets) **reflect** (bounce back) light from the Sun to Earth, the same way the construction paper reflects the light from the flashlight to the screen. Without the Sun, the Moon and planets would not shine.

LET'S EXPLORE

1. Different planets and other celestial bodies, such as moons, each reflect different amounts of light. How does the color of a reflecting material affect the amount of light reflected? Repeat the experiment, placing the white construction paper on the box as before. Observe the brightness of the light reflected on the screen. Then,

tape a different color paper, such as brown, over half of the white paper on the box. First, shine the light on the white paper, then on the brown paper, and compare the brightness of the light reflected on the screen by each paper. Repeat, using various colors, such as red, green, and black. From the results, determine how the surface or atmospheric color of a celestial body could affect its brightness in the sky.

2. How does distance affect a celestial body's **apparent brightness** (how bright a celestial body appears to be as observed from the Earth)? Repeat the original experiment, placing the box at different distances: 6 inches (15 cm), 12 inches (30 cm), and 18 inches (45 cm). Adjust the angle of the flashlight at each distance so that its light strikes the center of the construction paper on the box each time. Notice the screen's brightness at each distance. From the results, determine how distance from the Sun can affect a planet's apparent brightness.

SHOW TIME!

1. The reflecting ability of a celestial body is called its **albedo.** An albedo of 1.0 indicates 100 percent reflection. Design a table comparing the albedos of the nine planets: Earth (0.35), Jupiter (0.52), Mars (0.16), Mercury (0.1), Neptune (0.35), Pluto (0.5), Saturn (0.61), Uranus (0.35), Venus (0.76).

2. Celestial bodies not only reflect the light from the Sun, but can reflect sunlight onto other celestial bodies. Sunlight reflected off Earth is called **earthshine.** During the Moon's **crescent phase** (phase of the Moon with small lighted area resembling a segment of a ring with pointed ends), you can sometimes see the rest of the Moon's shape dimly lit as a result of earthshine.

To demonstrate the effect that earthshine has on the appearance of the Moon, divide a lemon-size piece of dark-colored clay in half and roll the two parts into balls. Stick one ball on the end of a craft stick. This ball will represent the Moon. Use the other ball to stand the Moon model on a table. Use books to raise a flashlight so that its bulb is about 2 inches (5 cm) from the backside (the side away from you) of the clay Moon. In a darkened room, observe the darkness of the front side of the Moon model. Move a cotton ball back and forth about 1 inch (2.5 cm) from the clay Moon. Observe the front side of the clay Moon as the cotton ball moves closer to it.

CHECK IT OUT!

Look at the Moon and you will see that some regions are darker than others. Early peoples imagined these shadowy areas were part of a human face, thus the saying "the man in the Moon." Find out more about the bright and dark features of the Moon. For information, see pages 6–9 in Fred Schaaf's *Seeing the Sky* (New York: Wiley, 1990).

Shadows

PROBLEM

How can the Moon block the Sun's light?

Materials

grape-size ball of clay
2 sharpened pencils
3-inch (7.5-cm) Styrofoam ball

Procedure

1. Place the ball of clay on the point of one of the pencils and the Styrofoam ball on the other pencil's point.

2. Hold the pencil with the Styrofoam ball at arm's length so that the ball is in front of your face.

3. Close one eye and hold the pencil with the clay ball in your other hand so that the ball is in front of, but not touching, your open eye. Slowly move the clay ball away from your face toward the Styrofoam ball. As you move the clay ball, observe how much of the Styrofoam ball is hidden by the clay ball at different distances.

Results

The closer the clay ball is to your face, the more it hides the Styrofoam ball.

Why?

The closer an object is to your eye, the bigger it appears. The small ball of clay can totally block your view of the larger Styrofoam ball. In the same way, the Moon with a diameter of 2,173 miles (3,476 km) can block our view of the much larger Sun, which has a diameter of 870,000 miles (1,392,000 km).

When the Moon passes directly between the Sun and Earth, and all three are in a straight line, the Moon **eclipses** (passes in front of and blocks the light of) the Sun. In this position, observers on Earth see a **solar eclipse.** The Sun is about 400 times larger than the Moon, but at times during the Moon's elliptical (oval shape) orbit, the Moon is about 400 times nearer Earth. It is in this position that the Moon and Sun appear to be the same size. In a solar eclipse in which the Moon appears as large as the Sun, the Moon completely covers the Sun, blocking all of its light. This event is called a **total solar eclipse.**

LET'S EXPLORE

When the Moon is far enough from Earth to appear smaller than the Sun, the Moon does not completely eclipse the Sun. An outer ring of the Sun's **photosphere** (bright visible surface of the Sun) is visible. This event is called an **annular eclipse.** Demonstrate an annular eclipse by repeating the experiment, slowly moving the clay ball away from your face until only a small outer ring of the Styrofoam ball is visible around the clay ball. **Science Fair Hint:** Make drawings to represent the Sun during the different types of solar eclipse.

SHOW TIME!

1. Like all shadows, the Moon's shadow consists of a dark inner region called the **umbra** and a lighter outer region called the **penumbra.** Observe these parts of a shadow by positioning a desk lamp as high as possible above a sheet of paper on the desk. Hold your hand under the lamp about 1 inch (2.5 cm) above the paper. Observe the inner and outer parts of your hand's shadow.

2. During a solar eclipse, only part of the Earth is in the shadow of the Moon. Observers in the umbra see a total solar eclipse, while those in the penumbra see a **partial solar eclipse** (only part of the Sun is blocked). Observers outside the Moon's shadow see no eclipse. Design a poster of a solar eclipse, similar to the one shown here, to show why a solar eclipse is not seen by all observers on the daytime side of the Earth.

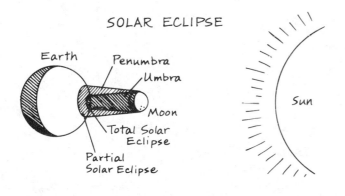

SOLAR ECLIPSE

3. Never look at the Sun with your naked eye. Viewing a solar eclipse can be dangerous if not done properly. Pinhole projection is one of the safest ways to observe a solar eclipse. To demonstrate this method, ask an adult to make a small hole in the center of an index card with the point of a pencil. This is the projector card. Darken the room except for a desk lamp. Point the bulb of the light outward and stand about 6 feet (1.8 m) in front of the bulb. With your back toward the light, hold the projec-

tor card so that the light passes through the hole to a second index card (the screen). Move the projector card back and forth toward the screen until the image of the light is seen on the screen. Ask a helper to slowly move a circle of black construction paper in front of the light. The black paper should be larger than the end of the lamp so that it totally covers it. When using this method to view a solar eclipse, keep your back to the Sun and watch the shadow on the screen. For more information about viewing a solar eclipse, see pages 24–36 in Philip S. Harrington's *Eclipse!* (New York: Wiley, 1997).

CHECK IT OUT!

Because the Earth rotates, during a total solar eclipse the small umbra of the Moon's shadow sweeps across the Earth's surface. Since the umbra is only about 167 miles (267 km) wide, a total eclipse of the Sun occurs rarely in any one spot on the Earth. Scientists can predict the location of future solar eclipses. For information about the dates and sites of future eclipses, see pages 686–687 in the *National Audubon Society Field Guide to the Night Sky* (New York: Alfred A. Knopf, 1995).

Biology

Building Blocks

PROBLEM

How can you make a model of an animal cell?

Materials

lemon gelatin dessert mix
1-quart (1-liter) resealable plastic bag
1-quart (1-liter) bowl
timer
large red grape
5 peanuts (with or without their shells)
adult helper
NOTE: This experiment requires a
  refrigerator.

Procedure

1. Have your adult helper prepare the gelatin dessert mix according to the instructions on the box.

2. Allow the gelatin to cool to room temperature.

3. Pour the gelatin into the resealable bag and seal the bag. Place the bag in the bowl.

4. Place the bowl in the refrigerator to chill until the gelatin is firm (about 3 to 4 hours).

5. When the gelatin is firm, remove the bowl from the refrigerator and open the bag.

6. Use your fingers to insert the grape into the center of the gelatin. Insert the peanuts in the gelatin so that they are distributed evenly throughout the gelatin.

7. Reseal the bag and place it on a flat surface, such as the kitchen counter. Observe its shape.

8. Hold the bag over the bowl and gently squeeze the bag. Do not squeeze so hard that the bag opens. Observe the shape of the bag as you squeeze.

Results

You have made a model of the four common parts of all cells.

Why?

A **cell** is the basic building block of organisms. (**Organisms** are all living things—people, plants, animals, and tiny living things called bacteria and fungi.) Animal cells differ in size and shape, but all have four common parts: a cell membrane, cytoplasm, mitochondria, and a nucleus. All four of these parts are represented in the model you made in this activity.

The plastic bag in your model represents the cell membrane. The **cell membrane** holds the cell together and protects the inner parts. The light-colored gelatin represents the grayish jellylike material, made mostly of water, called **cytoplasm** that fills the cell. The grape floating in the gelatin represents the nucleus. The **nucleus** is the control center that directs all the activities of the cell. The peanuts floating in the gelatin represent the "power stations" of the cell, called the **mitochondria.** In the mitochondria, food and **oxygen** (a gas in the air) combine to produce the energy needed for the cell to work and live.

The four common parts of an animal cell—cell membrane, cytoplasm, mitochondria, and nucleus—all work together and are necessary for the life of the cell. Like the basic model, many animal cells change shape when pressure is applied.

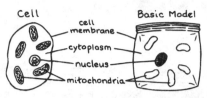

Cell
cell membrane
cytoplasm
nucleus
mitochondria

Basic Model

FOUR COMMON PARTS OF ALL CELLS

LET'S EXPLORE

1. How are plant cells different on the inside from animal cells? One way is that most plant cells contain chloroplasts. **Chloroplasts** are green bodies in plant cells that give plants their green color and in which food for the plant is made. Repeat the experiment, using 6 to 10 green grapes in addition to the red grape and peanuts. Insert the green grapes in the gelatin so that they are scattered throughout the gelatin. Do the grapes affect how the bag changes shape when at rest or when you squeeze it? Keep this model of the basic parts inside a plant cell for the next experiment.

2. Since plants do not have bones, what gives them support and shape? Set the cell model from the previous experiment in a small box, such as a shoe box. Observe any change in the shape of the box as you place it on a flat surface or squeeze it. The box represents the stiff outer layer of a plant cell, called the **cell wall.** By placing the bag of gelatin, which represents the basic parts inside a plant cell, inside the box, you now have a basic model of a plant cell. **Science Fair Hint:** Place the plant cell model on a flat surface and take a photograph. Photograph the basic model of the four common parts of all cells from the original experiment on the same flat surface. Display these photos to demonstrate the support that a cell wall gives to a plant cell.

SHOW TIME!

1. A **tissue** is a group of cells that perform a similar task. Demonstrate the difference between a plant cell and plant tissue by making five basic plant cell models, using the previous procedure. Put the lid on each box. Place two of the cell model boxes on top of two others to create two stacks, each two cells high. Place the fifth box near the two stacks. Fold two index cards in half. Label one card Plant Tissue and stand it in front of the two stacks. Label the other card Plant Cell and stand it in front of the fifth box. Display the boxes and photograph them. Use the photographs to prepare a poster to represent the difference between a plant cell and plant tissue.

2. **Organs** are structures consisting of different tissues grouped together to perform a specific function or functions. Plants have several organs. **Leaves** are organs for manufacturing food. **Roots** are organs that **absorb** (take in) and **transport** (to carry from one place to another) water and minerals. **Stems** are organs that support other organs such as leaves and **flowers** (organs for producing more plants). Find out more about these and other plant organs. For information, see *Janice VanCleave's Plants.* (New York: Wiley, 1997). Create and display a chart showing the different plant organs.

4 Reflectors

PROBLEM

Why are plant leaves green?

Materials

manila file folder
sheet of white office paper
paper clip
flashlight
sheet of green construction paper or any
    bright green paper
ruler
helper

Procedure

1. Open the file folder slightly and stand it on a table.

2. Attach the white paper to one side of the standing folder with the paper clip. The white paper will be called the screen.

3. Lay the flashlight alongside the standing folder. Rotate the flashlight so that the lamp end faces away from the screen at a 45-degree (45°) angle.

4. Fold the green paper in half lengthwise (long end to long end) to make it easier to hold.

5. Hold the green paper about 4 inches (10 cm) from the lamp end of the flashlight.

6. Turn on the flashlight, then ask your helper to darken the room.

7. Observe the color of the screen.

Results

The screen looks green.

Why?

The screen looks green because of something called pigment. **Pigments** are substances that absorb, reflect, and **transmit** (pass through) visible light. **Visible light** is made up of colors that can be seen by the human eye, commonly referred to as rainbow colors: red, orange, yellow, green, blue, indigo, and violet. White light, such as sunlight or light from a flashlight, is made up of the seven colors of visible light. When white light meets **matter** (the substance of which any object is made), any number of the different colors of light may be reflected, transmitted, or absorbed.

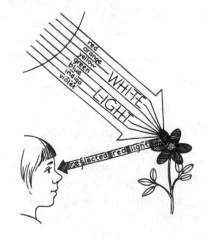

When a pigment is illuminated, or brightened, with white light, the color you see is the color of light reflected and/or transmitted by the pigment. (The rest of the colors of light are absorbed.) You see green on the screen because the pigment in the colored paper reflects green light. Similarly, you see green when looking at a green leaf because a pigment in the leaf called chlorophyll reflects and transmits green light. **Chlorophyll** is a green pigment located in the chloroplasts of plants. Chlorophyll is necessary in the process by which plants produce food, called **photosynthesis.** During photosynthesis, plants use light energy trapped by chlorophyll to change water and a gas in the air called **carbon dioxide** into food.

LET'S EXPLORE

When white light strikes a red flower, the flower absorbs all the colors in the white light except red. The flower appears red because only red light is reflected. Demonstrate this by repeating the experiment, using red paper. **Science Fair Hint:** Construct and use a diagram like the one shown as part of a project display.

SHOW TIME!

The colors of light that a pigment absorbs and transmits can be determined by an instrument called a **spectrophotometer.** Make a simple spectrophotometer by laying a sheet of white paper on a table. The sheet of paper will be your screen. Prepare a liquid containing pigment from a leaf, such as a geranium leaf, by tearing the leaf into small pieces and placing them in a clear plastic cup. Add 3 tablespoons (45 ml) of rubbing alcohol to the cup. *CAUTION: Keep the alcohol away from your nose and mouth.* Stir the contents of the cup as often as possible for 1 hour, then remove the pieces of leaf.

Hold the cup about 4 inches (10 cm) above the screen, and the flashlight about 2 inches (5 cm) above the cup. Shine the light through the liquid in the cup and onto the screen. The color seen on the screen is the color transmitted by the pigment removed from the leaf. The colors absorbed are all the colors making up white light, minus the transmitted and any reflected colors. Take a color photograph or make a color diagram to represent the results. Find out how professional spectrophotometers work.

CHECK IT OUT!

There are three groups of pigment in plants: chlorophyll, carotenoids, and phycobilins. Find out more about these pigments. Which colors does each group absorb, reflect, and transmit?

Up or Down?

PROBLEM

How does gravity affect plant growth of pinto beans?

Materials

paper towel
tap water
4 pinto beans
rubber band
masking tape
8-inch (20-cm) -square piece of cardboard
permanent marking pen
1-gallon (4-liter) resealable plastic bag

Procedure

1. Fold the paper towel in half three times, then moisten the folded paper towel with water.

2. Place the beans on the wet towel, evenly spaced as shown.

3. Fold one end of the paper towel over the first bean. Continue folding the towel end-over-end to form a roll around the beans.

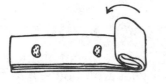

4. Wrap the rubber band around the bean roll.

5. Tape the bean roll to the center of the cardboard.

6. Draw an arrow on the cardboard above one of the open ends of the bean roll.

7. Place the cardboard inside the plastic bag so that the arrow points toward the open end of the bag. Seal the bag.

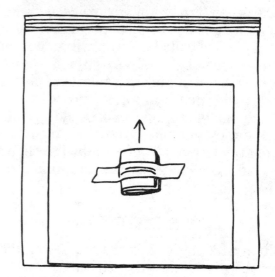

8. Tape the bag in an upright position to any stationary vertical object that allows a good view of the bag, such as a window.

9. Observe the bean roll as often as possible during each day for 7 days or until roots and stems extend from the end(s) of the bean roll.

Results

The stems of the plants in the bean roll grow upward and the roots grow downward.

Why?

Plants grow in certain directions because of the plant chemical **auxin.** Auxin makes plant cells elongate. The longer cells on one side then cause the plant to bend toward the shorter side. Different types of cells respond differently to the presence of this chemical. An increase in auxin increases the growth of stem cells, but inhibits the growth of root cells.

Gravity pulls auxin down toward the lowest part of the stems and roots of a plant. More growth occurs in the cells on the lower side of the stem, and less growth in the cells on the lower side of the root. The result is that the stem bends up and the roots bend down. The growth response of plants to gravity is called **geotropism.** Since stems grow in a direction opposite to the pull of gravity, they have a **negative geotropism,** while roots have a **positive geotropism.**

LET'S EXPLORE

Do stems and roots continue to be affected by gravity as they grow? Repeat the experiment, preparing 4 bean roll bags. Use a protractor to draw a 6-inch (15-cm) -diameter circle on the cardboard in each bag. Make a mark every 10° around each circle. When the stems are about 2 inches (5 cm) long, change the position of three of the bags so that the arrows on the bags point down, right, and left. Let the fourth bag, the control bag, remain with its arrow pointing up. Make daily observations for 7 days, using the circles to compare the change in the direction of each plant's stems and roots. **Science Fair Hint:** Take photographs to represent the procedure and results of the experiment.

SHOW TIME!

1a. Most plants grow on the side of a hill in the same up-and-down direction as plants on a flat surface. Demonstrate this by filling a shallow pan with about 2 inches (5 cm) of potting soil. Plant 6 to 8 pinto beans in the soil, and moisten the soil with water. Stand a toothpick in the soil vertically next to each bean. Prop up one end

of the pan by placing a ball of clay at each corner. When the shoots emerge, use a protractor each day to measure the angle between the shoots and the toothpicks.

b. Repeat the experiment, using seeds of different plants, such as squash, cucumber, lima bean, or corn. Use toothpicks of different colors to identify the different seeds used.

2. Does gravity affect the growth of mature plants? With an adult's permission, lay a small houseplant on its side in a dark closet or under a cardboard box to prevent it from responding to light. Observe the position of the stems and leaves after 1 week and again 1 week later. Add water as needed to keep the soil moist. At the end of 3 weeks, carefully remove the soil from around the roots and observe their direction in relationship to the direction of the stems. Take a photograph of the plant at the beginning of the experiment and each time you observe the plant.

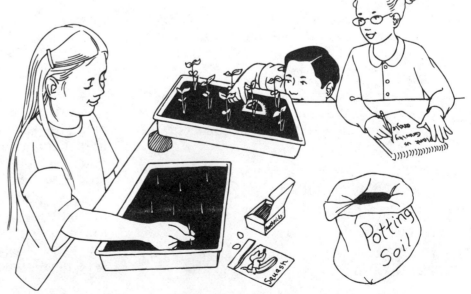

With and Without

PROBLEM

Is light on the soil needed for mustard seed germination?

Materials

pencil
3 egg cartons (polystyrene, not paper)
scissors
3 cups (750 ml) potting soil
mustard seeds
1-tablespoon (15-ml) measuring spoon
tap water

Procedure

1. Use the following steps to construct a closable germinating tray:

   • Use the pencil to punch a small drainage hole in the bottom of each compartment of one of the egg cartons.

   • Cut the lid off a second carton. Discard the bottom of the carton. *NOTE: Recycle discarded polystyrene.*

   • Set the first egg carton in the lid of the second carton so that the lid will catch water draining through the holes.

2. Construct an open germinating tray from the third egg carton. Repeat the previous procedure, but remove the lid from the egg carton and use that lid to collect drain water.

3. Fill the compartments of both germinating trays about half full with soil.

4. Sprinkle a few mustard seeds in each compartment of the trays.

5. Cover the seeds with about 1 tablespoon (15 ml) of soil.

6. Moisten the soil in each tray with an equal amount of water. Keep the soil in each tray moist, but not wet, during the entire experiment.

7. Close the lid of the first germinating tray. Place both trays near a window that receives light most of the day, such as a window facing south.

8. Observe the open tray daily for the first signs of plant growth.

Results

The seeds in both trays germinate.

Why?

During the last stages of seed development, the seed **dehydrates** (loses water) until it contains very little water. The **embryo** (partially developed plant inside a seed) ceases to grow and remains inactive until the seed germinates. Thus, **germination** doesn't mean that a seed comes alive, but rather that the embryo resumes growth and development that stopped during the last stages of seed development.

Mustard is a **dicot,** meaning it is an **angiosperm** (flowering plant) and its seeds have two **cotyledons** (seed leaves). Some dicot seeds, such as mustard, germinate as soon as they are in favorable conditions. Favorable conditions for mustard seeds are sufficient warmth, water, and oxygen. All the seeds in this experiment were exposed to light before being planted. Since the seeds grew in the closed tray, light on the soil was not needed for the seeds to germinate.

LET'S EXPLORE

1a. Would other dicots give the same results? Repeat the experiment, planting dicot seeds such as radish or beans. Make diagrams of both trays, indicating which type of seed is in each compartment. **Science Fair Hint:** Continue to make diagrams of the seeds in each tray throughout the experiment to use as part of a project display.

b. Would not covering the seeds with soil affect the result? Repeat the previous experiment, filling the containers with soil. Press the seeds into the surface of the soil, but do not cover them with soil.

Use a magnifying lens to observe and study the seeds daily.

c. Would **monocot** (angiosperm whose seeds have one cotyledon) seeds give the same results? Repeat the previous experiments using corn kernels.

SHOW TIME!

Does the depth that the seeds are planted affect the results? Fill two 10-ounce (300-ml) clear plastic cups with soil. In each cup, plant 4 to 5 pinto beans at different depths so that they are visible through the side of the cup. Place one bean on the surface of the soil. Moisten the soil in each cup with water and keep the soil moist during the experiment. Set the cups near a window. Turn a large Styrofoam cup upside down and use it to cover one of the cups. Observe the seeds daily, quickly lifting and replacing the lid of the covered cup in order to limit the amount of light entering the cup. Display dated photographs and/or drawings of the seeds to represent the results.

CHECK IT OUT!

Some seeds will not germinate until they are exposed to light before planting. Plowing a field or cultivating the soil in a garden usually results in plant growth, partly because turning the soil exposes the seeds in the soil to light. Find out more about the effect of light on seed germination. Does the color of light affect germination? For a method of discovering the effect of different colors of light, see page 79 in *Janice VanCleave's Plants.* (Wiley: New York, 1997).

Getting Started

PROBLEM

How long does it take a pinto bean to begin growing?

Materials

paper towels
10-ounce (300-ml) clear plastic cup
6 pinto beans
tap water
magnifying lens

Procedure

1. Fold a paper towel in half and use it to line the inside of the cup.

2. Crumple several paper towels together and stuff them into the cup. Use enough towels to hold the paper lining firmly in place around the inside of the cup.

3. Place the beans between the cup and the lining, spacing the beans evenly around the **perimeter** (the measurement of a boundary) of the cup.

4. Moisten the paper towels in the cup with water. Keep the paper towels in the cup moist, but not dripping wet, during the entire experiment.

5. Use the magnifying lens to observe the beans two or three times daily until you see growth. This will occur within 4 to 5 days.

Results

The first signs of growth is the appearance of the beak-shaped **hypocotyl** (the part of a plant embryo that develops into roots).

Why?

The process by which a seed develops is called germination. In the experiments in this book, the time it takes from planting a seed to the first signs of growth is called germination starting time (GST).

LET'S EXPLORE

1. Do **nutrients** (materials needed for the life and growth of living organisms) affect GST? Repeat the experiment, preparing 2 cups of beans. Wet the paper towels in one cup with distilled water and those in the other cup with liquid commercial plant fertilizer. Prepare the fertilizer by doubling the water in the instructions on the package.

2. Pinto beans are dicots. Is GST the same for other dicots? Repeat the original experiment, using different kinds of dicot seeds, such as peas, squash, or zinnia. **Science Fair Hint:** Use drawings or photos of each seed type to create a display that represents the GST results for each.

3. Does light affect GST? Repeat the original experiment, preparing 2 cups of beans. Cover one of the cups with a sheet of black construction paper wrapped around the cup. Fold and staple the top and sides of the paper. Observe the beans two to three times a day until the first signs of growth are seen. Lift the paper covering to observe the beans in the covered cup.

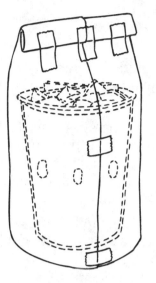

SHOW TIME!

In this book, the time it takes from planting a seed to the end of germination is called **germination time** (GT). GT is determined by the time it takes for the **epicotyl** (part of a plant embryo that develops into stems, leaves, flowers, and fruit) to fully emerge. Does the depth the seed is planted affect GT? Place a piece of masking tape down the side of 3 cups. Label the cups 1, 2, and 3. Place 2 seeds in the bottom of cup 1. Fill cup 2 about one-fourth full with soil, and place 2 beans on the surface of the soil. Fill cup 3 about one-half full with soil, and place 2 beans on the soil. Fill each cup three-fourths full with soil. The height of the soil in each cup must be the same. Keep the soil moist, but not wet, throughout the experiment.

CHECK IT OUT!

Seeds remain *dormant* (inactive) until certain conditions exist. For example, the seeds of some desert plants contain chemicals that prevent germination. The seeds are able to grow only after sufficient rainfall washes away these chemicals. Find out more about the conditions for breaking the dormancy of different seeds.

Clipped

PROBLEM

How do grass stems grow?

Materials

masking tape
marking pen
ruler

NOTE: This experiment must be performed outdoors in an area of tall grass, such as johnsongrass.

Procedure

CAUTION: Take precautions to protect yourself from insect bites.

1. Choose a stem of tall grass, but do not pick it. Attach a small piece of tape to the tip of the stem. Write the number 1 on the tape to identify the stem.

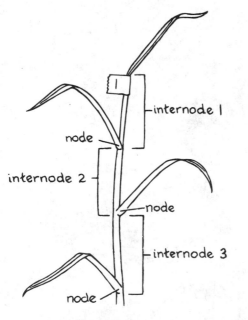

2. Locate the nodes on the stem. (The nodes are the thickened areas where the blades of grass branch off the stem.)

3. Starting at the tip of the stem, measure and record the length of three or more internodes (the area between two consecutive nodes). Call the internode at the tip of the stem internode 1.

4. Repeat step 3, using two other stems of grass. Attach a small piece of tape to the tip of each stem. Write the numbers 2 and 3 on the pieces of tape to identify these two stems.

5. Wait 2 days, then measure and record the length of each internode on all three stems.

Results

Each internode increases in length.

Why?

Upright grass stems aboveground are called **culms** and are made of two parts: nodes and internodes. **Nodes** are solid **joints** (where parts fit together) where leaves are generally attached. The **internodes**, or areas between the nodes, are usually hollow, but may be **pithy** (soft and spongy) or solid. Generally, stems of dicot plants grow at their tips. But stems of many monocots, such as grasses, grow just above each node along the stem. When an upper section of a grass stem is cut off, the lower part of the stem continues to grow. This type of growth allows grass to survive being clipped off by lawn mowers or nibbled to the ground by various animals.

LET'S EXPLORE

Is there a difference in the amount of growth of different internodes on a grass stem? Use the measurements from the

Grass Stem 1

Internode number	Final length	Minus	Starting length	Equals	Growth
1	6 inches (15 cm)	–	4 inches (10 cm)	=	2 inches (5 cm)

experiment to construct a data chart similar to the one shown. Use the chart shown to determine the differences in the amount of growth of the internodes.

SHOW TIME!

1. Is there growth both above and below a node on a grass stem? Use two pieces of masking tape about 2 inches (5 cm) long for each node in this experiment. Attach one piece of tape to the stem directly above a node, and a second piece of tape directly below the same node. Write the number 1 on both pieces of tape. Repeat the procedure, attaching two more pieces of tape above and below a second node on the same stem. Write the number 2 on these two pieces of tape. Each day for 3 or more days, measure the distance from each piece of tape to each corresponding node.

2. Does the entire internode on a grass stem grow? Choose one stem of johnsongrass or other tall grass, then use a marking pen to mark four equal sections on an internode. Mark a few more internodes in the same way. Measure and record the distance between the marks once a day for 2 days.

3. Do short grasses, such as lawn grasses, grow the same way that tall grasses do? With an adult's permission, use a spade to dig up a clump of short grass large enough to fit inside a paper cup. Choose a clump that has at least three stems, and get as many of the grass roots as possible. Plant the grass in a cup of soil. Moisten the soil with water and keep it moist throughout the experiment.

   Choose one stem. Starting at the tip of the stem, use a marking pen to mark three equal sections on an internode. Mark at least two more internodes in the same way. Measure and record the distance between the marks once a day for 7 days.

CHECK IT OUT!

Grasses, such as Bermuda grass, have creeping stems that grow below and above ground. Find out more about grass stems. What are rhizomes? Stolons?

3-D

PROBLEM

How can you make a model of an adult insect's main body parts?

Materials

4-ounce (113-g) stick of clay
sheet of paper
ruler
table knife
round toothpick
pencil
4-by-8-inch (10-by-20-cm) unruled index
   card

Procedure

1. Lay the clay on the paper. Roll it into a tube 6 inches (15 cm) long.

2. Use the knife to cut the clay roll into three pieces: 1 inch (2.5 cm), 2 inches (5 cm), and 3 inches (7.5 cm) long.

3. Round the end of each piece of clay.

4. Break the toothpick in half. Use one half of the toothpick to connect the 1-inch (2.5-cm) piece of clay to the 2-inch (5-cm) piece. Push the two clay pieces together so they touch.

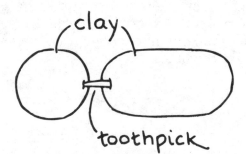

5. Use the remaining half of the toothpick to connect the 3-inch (7.5-cm) piece of clay to the free end of the 2-inch (5-cm) piece. Push the clay pieces together as before.

6. Lay the connected clay on the paper and mold into the shape of an insect's body as shown in the diagram.

7. Use the point of the pencil to carve two shallow grooves around the middle clay section, dividing it into three parts. Carve nine shallow grooves around the large end section, dividing it into ten parts.

8. Place the clay model on the index card and label the parts as shown.

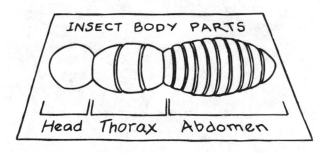

Results

You have made a three-dimensional model of an insect's main body parts.

Why?

The body of an adult **insect** is divided into three main body parts: the head, the thorax, and the abdomen. The head is the front part. The **thorax** is the middle part, which is divided into 3 smaller segments. The **abdomen** is the rear part, which is divided into 10 or fewer smaller segments. Every insect has the same three body parts, with the abdomen and thorax divided into 13 or fewer segments.

LET'S EXPLORE

1a. Eyes, **mouthparts** (body parts used to gather and eat food), and **antennae** (movable body parts used to smell, feel, and sometimes to hear) are located on the insect's head. Find out about the number, size, and exact location of these parts. Repeat the activity to prepare the head and thorax, but do not connect them. Set the thorax aside for the following activities.

Design ways to make models of the eyes, mouthparts, and antennae on the clay head, such as by using pipe cleaners for antennae and balls of clay for eyes. Insert differently colored toothpicks at each head part location and make a color-keyed legend of the toothpicks. **Science Fair Hint:** Display the head model on a separate index card with labels and legends.

b. One pair of jointed (consisting of different parts that fit together) legs is attached to each of the three sections of an insect's thorax, one on each side. Each leg has four main parts, from the **coxa** connected to the body, to the **femur, tibia,** and **tarsus** at the outermost end of the leg. Observe an insect to determine the approximate length of each leg segment. Use pipe cleaners to represent legs. Attach the legs to the thorax and bend the pipe cleaners to show each leg segment.

c. Insect wings, when present, are in pairs. If only one pair is present, it is attached to the middle thorax segment. But most insects have two pairs of wings. The second pair is attached to the third thorax segment. Find out the length of insect wings and add wing models to the clay thorax. Make wing models by cutting them from waxed paper. Tape a toothpick to one end of each wing and insert the toothpicks in the clay.

SHOW TIME!

Most adult insects have wings. Insect wings vary in number, size, shape, texture, **veins** (framework of thickened ridges), and

position at which they are held at rest. The number and arrangement of veins are used to identify insects. Some insects, such as flies, have two wings. Most winged adult insects, like butterflies, moths, dragonflies, wasps, and bees, have four wings. Most insect wings are **membranous** (resembling a thin, flexible sheet of tissue paper) and may have tiny hairs or scales. Some insects, such as beetles, have thick, leathery, or even hard front wings.

Use a field guide to find out more about insect wings and design different models. Display the models with drawings or pictures of the insect that has each wing type. Use waxed paper for transparent wings. Draw the veins on these wings with a permanent marker. Construction paper can be used to form thick wings.

CHECK IT OUT!

Insects have a heart and blood, but no blood vessels. Find out more about insects' internal body parts. How does their blood circulate? How can models of an insect's internal body parts be made?

Face Forward

PROBLEM

What type of vision do animals have if their eyes face forward?

Materials

2 sheets of notebook paper
cellophane tape

Procedure

1. Roll each sheet of paper into a 1-inch (2.5-cm) tube. Fasten the edge of the paper with cellophane tape.

2. Hold the tubes to your eyes as you would a pair of binoculars.

3. Keep both eyes open.

4. While looking through both tubes, slowly move the far ends of the tubes together until you see one clear image of the object being viewed.

5. Close your left eye, and make note of what your right eye sees through the tube.

6. Close your right eye, and make note of what your left eye sees through the tube.

Results

Each eye does not see exactly the same thing. The right eye views more of the right side of the object, and the left eye views more of the left side of the object.

Why?

A **predator** (an animal that hunts and kills other animals for its food) has its eyes facing forward on the front of its head like your own eyes. In this position, objects are viewed from two different angles. The two images are projected on the **retina** (back portion of the eye) where they overlap. The overlapping images are interpreted by the brain as one clear, three-dimensional picture. The ability to combine images viewed by two eyes is called **binocular vision.**

LET'S EXPLORE

A chameleon's eyes face forward, but the eyes can move independently of each other when searching for food. What might the world look like through the roving eyes of a chameleon? Move the far ends of the tubes in different directions—up and down, left and right. Observe and record what you see. You should know that when this animal prepares to take aim with its tongue to capture its prey, the eyes face forward, giving the animal good distance judgment.

LEFT EYE VIEW

RIGHT EYE VIEW

SHOW TIME!

1. How does binocular vision produce a three-dimensional view? Discover how the overlapping of two images produces a three-dimensional picture by holding this book so that the tip of your nose touches the dot in the diagram. Keep both eyes open. Look straight forward as you slowly turn the book in a counterclockwise direction and watch the car travel up the path. Design other diagrams and use them as part of a project display. Make sample copies for project observers to turn so that they can see the objects move.

2. How good is your **peripheral vision** (your sideview vision)? Your eyes, like those of other animals with eyes facing forward, have about a 180-degree angle of vision. Test your peripheral vision by standing in the center of a circle. Ask a helper to start from a point on the circle behind you and

to slowly walk around the circle. Continue to look forward, not moving your eyes to the right or left. Make a mark on the circle when you first see your helper and again when he or she moves out of view on the opposite side. Test the angle of peripheral vision of other people. Photographs taken during this experiment can be used as part of your project display.

CHECK IT OUT!

Horses have eyes so placed that they can see all around their heads. The eyes of owls remain stationary, but their heads rotate 180°, so they, too, can view the entire world around them. It is difficult to sneak up on an animal that sees from all angles. Discover more about the position of animal eyes and how this position affects an animal's life.

"Hearing" Without Ears

PROBLEM

How do newts and salamanders hear without external ears?

Materials

metal pie pan
table salt
metal spoon

Procedure

1. Place the pie pan upside down on a table.

2. Sprinkle a very thin layer of salt over the upturned bottom of the pan.

3. Tap on the upturned bottom of the pan with the spoon.

4. Observe and record any difference in the movement of the salt crystals.

Results

Tapping on the pan causes the salt crystals to move around.

Why?

The molecules in the pan that is struck by the spoon start to **vibrate** (quickly move back and forth). As these molecules move, they bump into neighboring molecules and start them moving, but with slightly less energy. This continues until there just is not enough energy to cause the neighboring molecules to vibrate. Newts and salamanders that walk on land are able to "hear" by feeling vibrations from the surface they stand on. A slender muscle connects the **scapula** (shoulder blade) to bones set in a thin membrane of the ear cavity in the head. The vibrations from the surface travel up the bone in the front leg to the scapula, through the muscle, and on to the ear. **Sounds** (vibrations traveling through materials) close to the animal produce stronger vibrations, just like the greater movement of the salt crystals close to the tapping.

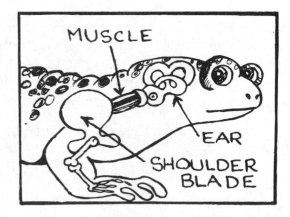

MUSCLE
EAR
SHOULDER BLADE

SALT

LET'S EXPLORE

1. Does the surface being tapped affect the vibrations? Repeat the experiment by placing the salt grains on different surfaces—a cardboard box, a wooden table, a plastic dish.

2. How does the distance from the tapped area affect the vibrations? Repeat the experiment tapping on the side of the pan farther from where the salt crystals are spread.

SHOW TIME!

1. How do other creatures without external ears, like fish, "hear"? Fish have a lateral line that runs down the side of their body. This line of **nerves** (special bundles of cells that the body uses to carry messages to and from the brain) can detect the pressure of sound that travels through the water. Demonstrate the movement of waves through water by pouring 1 inch (2.5 cm) of water into a rectangular glass baking dish. Place the dish under a desk lamp and gently touch the surface of the water. Observe and record the movement of the water. Tap on the side of the dish, and determine if the sound is transmitted through the water. Display photographs of the experiment as part of your project.

2. Birds have a keen sense of hearing. Owls can hear and locate their prey in the dark. The robin seems to be able to hear the movement of earthworms underground. Discover more about the ability of birds to receive sound. Display pictures of birds along with any unusual hearing abilities you have noted.

CHECK IT OUT!

Elephants have very large ears and are able to hear faint sounds. Donkeys have the ability to move their ears and are alerted by the slightest noise. Discover more about the size and shape of external ears and how they affect the ability to hear.

Oops!

PROBLEM

How long does it take you to catch a falling object?

Materials

table and chair
helper
ruler

Procedure

1. Sit on the chair with your forearm on the tabletop and your writing hand extending over the edge of the tabletop.

2. Ask your helper to hold the ruler so that the bottom of the stick (the zero end) is just above your hand.

3. Place your thumb and index finger on either side of, but not touching, the bottom of the ruler.

4. Ask your helper to drop the ruler through your fingers without telling you when it is going to be dropped.

5. After the ruler is released, try to catch it as quickly as possible between your thumb and fingers.

6. Observe the number on the ruler just above your thumb. Record this number as the reaction distance.

Results

The distance the ruler falls varies with each individual.

Why?

Reaction time is the time it takes you to respond to a situation. In this experiment, your reaction time was how long it took you to catch the falling ruler. The greater the reaction time, the greater is the reaction distance. In this project, the reaction distance will be used as the reaction time. Reaction distance will vary with individuals because when the ruler begins to fall, a message is sent to the brain. Like a computer, the brain takes this input information and, in fractions of a second, sends a message telling the muscles in the hand to contract. The distance the ruler falls can be different for each individual because it depends on the time it takes for these messages to be sorted out by the brain and the output message to be received by the hand's muscles. Nerves carry these messages. The nerves in the eye start this relay of messages. The first stop is in the largest section of the brain called the **cerebrum.** The cerebrum is where all thoughts occur and where input from sensory nerves is interpreted. The cerebrum sends a message (nerve impulse) to another section of the brain called the **cerebellum.** The cerebellum brings together all the muscle actions that are necessary to grasp the ruler. This does not have anything to do with how smart you are; instead it compares differences in eye-hand coordination.

LET'S EXPLORE

1. Would practice change the reaction time? Repeat the experiment ten times. Record the reaction distance for each trial in a chart similar to the one shown here. Plot

the data on a graph, labeling the graph Reaction Time and using reaction distances in inches (centimeters) as the reaction time.

Wade's Data Chart

Trial Number	Reaction Distance	Trial Number	Reaction Distance
1	18 inches (45 cm)	6	11 inches (28 cm)
2	14 inches (36 cm)	7	10 inches (25 cm)
3	12 inches (30 cm)	8	9 inches (23 cm)
4	12 inches (30 cm)	9	9 inches (23 cm)
5	11 inches (28 cm)	10	8 inches (20 cm)

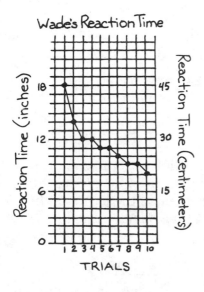

Wade's Reaction Time

2. Would using a different hand affect the results? Change hands and repeat the experiment. Compare the differences in the improvement of the reaction times for the two hands.

3. Would distractions affect the results? Have a second helper to ask questions during the experiment. The questions could be simple math problems or anything that requires enough thinking to be distracting. Compare the reaction times with and without distractions.

4. Does the age of the experimenter affect the reaction time? Ask people of different ages to perform the experiment. **Science Fair Hint:** Photographs taken during the experiment along with graphs representing the results can be displayed.

SHOW TIME!

Can the reaction time of animals other than humans be influenced? Find out how dogs, horses, whales, and other animals are trained. A report about training animals can be part of a project. Include in the report answers to such questions as:

- What stimuli are used to encourage these animals to respond?

- Which animals respond the fastest?

All living organisms are constantly responding to stimuli around them. **Stimuli** are things that cause a response in a living organism. A cat hears a bird chirping, and its ears send a message to the brain. The cat may respond to the stimulus (the bird's chirp) in different ways—raising its ears, twitching its tail, or standing alert. Observe and discover other common responses made by animals around you. A diagram, like the one for the cat, can be used to represent the stimulus-response behavior of the animals.

CHECK IT OUT!

How do drugs and alcohol affect reaction time? Good sources for information about the effects of drugs would be your teacher, parent, school nurse, and/or physician.

13

Juicy

PROBLEM

How do flies eat?

Materials

eyedropper
jar of sweet-potato baby food
craft stick
masking tape
pen
NOTE: This experiment requires a refrigerator.

Procedure

1. Place the tip of the eyedropper just below the surface of the potatoes in the jar. Try to fill the eyedropper with the sweet potatoes. Observe the amount of sweet potatoes that enter the eyedropper, if any.

2. Wash the eyedropper and allow it to dry.

3. Collect as much saliva in your mouth as possible, put the saliva on the craft stick, and transfer the saliva to the surface of the potatoes in the jar. Close the jar.

4. Place a piece of tape across the lid and down the sides of the jar. Label the tape DO NOT EAT.

5. Place the jar in the refrigerator and leave it undisturbed for 1 day.

6. After 24 hours, remove the jar from the refrigerator and repeat step 1.

Results

On your first try, you can draw little or no potatoes into the eyedropper. After the saliva has been in the jar for 24 hours, the potatoes at the surface are liquid. You can then easily draw them into the eyedropper.

Why?

Human saliva, like the saliva of flies and many other insects, contains a chemical called **amylase.** Amylase breaks down **starch,** a complex chemical found in many foods, into less complex chemicals. When humans eat food containing starch, amylase in the saliva begins to **digest** (break down into useable forms) the starch in the food. In the experiment, the amylase in your saliva digested the potatoes, turning them to liquid. The digesting process started as soon as the saliva touched the food, but it took 24 hours for enough liquid to form for you to be able to draw it into the eyedropper.

As you did in the experiment, flies drop saliva on the food they plan to eat. The amylase in the fly saliva quickly begins to digest the starch in the food. The fly dabs at the liquefied food with the end of its tubelike mouthpart called a **proboscis.** The spongy end of the proboscis soaks up the liquid. The liquid food then moves through the proboscis into the insect's digestive system, where the food is further broken down and the nourishing parts are absorbed by the body.

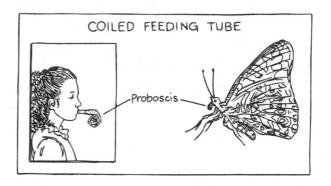

COILED FEEDING TUBE

Proboscis

LET'S EXPLORE

Potatoes, rice, and pasta are all starchy foods. Can amylase in fly saliva dissolve nonstarchy foods? Repeat the experiment using jars of nonstarchy foods, such as chicken, meat, or spinach.

SHOW TIME!

1. Butterflies and moths use the proboscis to reach the sweet **nectar** (sugary liquid) of flowers. The proboscis stays coiled under the head of the butterfly or moth when not in use. Blood from the insect's body is forced into the proboscis, causing the proboscis to uncoil. When uncoiled, the proboscis is used by the insect to suck up nectar.

Demonstrate the coiling and uncoiling of a proboscis with a party blower. Place the party blower upside down in your mouth so that the end hangs down and coils toward your body. Blow into the tube, then suck the air out. Have someone take photos of you with the blower coiled and uncoiled. Prepare posters comparing photos of the coiled and uncoiled party blower with drawings of a butterfly's proboscis.

2. Different insects have different types of mouthparts. Observe the plierlike mouth of a cricket. Catch a cricket and place it in a plastic resealable vegetable bag with a small piece of bread and a small piece of sponge moistened with water. Use a magnifying lens to observe how the cricket eats the food. Within 60 minutes, release the cricket where you found it.

Find out more about the different mouthparts of insects. Prepare a display using materials to represent each mouthpart type, such as pliers for a cricket, a coiled party blower for a butterfly, and a sponge for a fly.

CHECK IT OUT!

Insects take food into their body through their mouthparts. Through digestion, the food is chemically changed to supply the body with *nutrients* (substances used by the body for growth, repair, and energy) and get rid of any waste products. Find out more about how insects digest food. What is a crop? A gizzard? For information, see pages 48–51 in *Janice VanCleave's Insects* (New York: Wiley, 1998).

Break Out

PROBLEM

What happens to the exoskeleton of a growing insect?

Materials

12-inch (30-cm) round balloon
spring-type clothespin
1 tablespoon (15 ml) school glue
1 tablespoon (15 ml) tap water
small bowl
spoon
35 to 40 newspaper strips, each about 2 × 4 inches (5 × 10 cm)

Procedure

1. Blow up the balloon to about the size of a grapefruit.

2. Twist the end closed and secure it with the clothespin.

3. Put the glue and the water in the bowl and mix them by stirring with the spoon.

4. Dip a newspaper strip in the glue mixture and stick the strip on the balloon.

5. Repeat this with a second paper strip, placing it on the balloon so that it overlaps half of the first paper strip.

6. Continue adding strips, overlapping each one until most of the balloon is covered with paper. Leave a narrow strip around the balloon uncovered.

7. Wait an hour or so until the paper dries.

8. Once the paper is dry, remove the clothespin without letting the air out. Gently blow into the balloon, making it slightly larger.

Results

A firm paper shell covers the balloon. When you blow up the balloon even more, the uncovered section of the paper shell separates.

Why?

The balloon and hard paper shell represent an insect during a growing stage. The body of the growing insect is covered by an **exoskeleton** (external skeleton). This exoskeleton does not grow with the insect. As the rest of the insect's body grows, the exoskeleton starts to become too small. A new exoskeleton begins to form under the old one.

When the old exoskeleton becomes too small for the growing insect, blood and sometimes air or water inside the insect is forced into the thorax by the **contraction** (squeezing together) of muscles in the abdomen. This splits the exoskeleton, usually along the middle of the back side, and the insect crawls out. This process of shedding the exoskeleton is called **molting.** Most insects molt four to eight times during their lives, but they typically do not molt or continue to grow in size once they reach the adult stage.

LET'S EXPLORE

When the insect first crawls out of its old exoskeleton, its new exoskeleton is still moist and flexible like the wet paper strips on the balloon. The insect gulps in air or water to expand the flexible exoskeleton before it dries and hardens like the paper strips. The dried, stretched exoskeleton provides growing space until the next molt.

Demonstrate the stretching of an insect's exoskeleton by repeating the experiment. While the glue is still wet, stand in front of a mirror and observe the paper covering as you slightly blow up the balloon. While the exoskeleton model is enlarged, twist the open end of the balloon and secure it with a clothespin. Allow the paper to dry, then let a little air out of the balloon. **Science Fair Hint:** Display diagrams showing the changes in the paper model of an exoskeleton.

SHOW TIME!

Mealworms are **darkling beetles** in a growing stage. Purchase a container of mealworms from a pet store.

NOTE: Mealworms are pests, so before purchasing them, make plans for their fate after the experiment. You can use them for food for a pet lizard or humanely kill them by placing their container in the freezer overnight.

Spread the contents of the container on a paper towel and look for exoskeletons that have been discarded by molting mealworms.

Sort the mealworms by length, placing them in three piles: short, medium, and long. Use three plastic containers with lids, such as empty, clean, 4-cup (1.36-kg) margarine containers, to house the three groups of mealworms. Fill each container about half full with cornmeal. Place a potato slice and mealworms on the surface of the cornmeal. Fold a paper towel in half twice and place it over the potato slice, mealworms, and cornmeal. Secure the lids, then make 10 to 15 airholes in each lid with the point of a pencil. Label the containers Small, Medium, and Large.

Place the containers on a tray. Set the tray in an area at room temperature and out of direct light. Observe the contents of each container every 2 to 3 days for 3 to 4 weeks. Measure and record the average length of the mealworms in each container. Record changes in the length of the mealworms and the number of exoskeletons you find. Observe the width of the mealworms and make note of any changes. *NOTE: Remove the old potato slice and add a new one each week.*

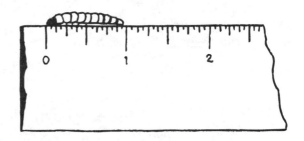

CHECK IT OUT!

Insects produce *hormones,* which are chemicals that control molting and other processes. The hormone that controls molting in immature insects is called *ecdysone.* For more information about molting hormones, see pages 29-33 of *Entomology* by H. Steven Dashefsky (New York: TAB Books, 1994). What does the juvenile hormone control?

Super Spout

PROBLEM

How can you model the content of a whale's spout?

Materials

hand mirror
freezer
paper towel

Procedure

1. Place the hand mirror in the freezer for 5 minutes.

2. Open the freezer, and observe any fog forming in front of the freezer.

3. Remove the mirror from the freezer.

4. Wipe the mirror with the dry paper towel.

5. Hold the mirror about 2 inches (5 cm) from your mouth.

6. Breathe onto the mirror.

7. Observe the surface of the mirror.

Results

The mirror becomes fogged with tiny droplets of water.

Why?

Air in your **lungs** (breathing organs) is warm and moist. The cooling of warm, moist air changes the water from a gas to a liquid. The process of a gas changing to a liquid is called **condensation.** The moisture in your exhaled breath **condenses** (changes from a gas to a liquid) when it hits the mirror's cool surface. When small amounts of warm moist air are cooled, small droplets of water are formed. A whale's body cavity acts as a giant air-storage tank. The condensing of such large amounts of warm, moist air upon exhaling results in a spout that looks like a geyser. The spray from the whale is a mixture of water and air.

LET'S EXPLORE

1. Would making the mirror colder affect the results? Repeat the experiment, but leave the mirror in the freezer for a longer period of time.

2. What effect would warming the mirror have on the results? Repeat the experiment, warming the mirror in sunlight.

SHOW TIME!

1. What causes the whale's spout to shoot so far into the air? Whales dive far below the water's surface. The weight of the water on the whale causes the air inside its body to compress, or get pushed into a small space. When the whale quickly surfaces and exhales, the gases expand and are pushed out with a great force. A spout of air and water shoots upward from the hole in the whale's head to about 50 feet (15 m).

This can be demonstrated by spraying some of the contents of a spray bottle filled with water into the air. Squeezing the handle pushes the water out with a great force in the same way that the air shoots from inside the whale's body. Diagrams showing the spray bottle and a whale's spout can be used as part of a science project display.

2. A whale can **exhale** (breathe out) as much as 2,000 quarts (2,000 liters) of air. How many quarts (liters) of air can a human exhale? A gallon plastic milk jug holds 4 quarts (4 liters). Use this jug to measure the amount of air that you can exhale. Fill the jug with water and turn it upside down into a pan of water. With the assistance of a helper, place one end of a clean aquarium tube inside the mouth of the jug. Breathe normally, and exhale through the other end of the tube. Measure and subtract the amount of water left in the jug from 4 quarts (4 liters) to determine the amount of air that you exhaled. As a display, you could use a picturegram to show the number of quarts exhaled by different animals.

3. The lungs of frogs are not very efficient. The frog's mouth acts as a bellows to pump air in and out of its lungs. Demonstrate this by exhaling and **inhaling** (breathing in) into a paper bag. Diagrams of the change in the bag's size as you exhale and inhale can be displayed and compared to changes in a frog's lungs.

CHECK IT OUT!

Respiration involves the exchanges of gases. Oxygen is the gas that enters the body cells, and carbon dioxide is the gas that leaves the cells. In animals with lungs, this gas exchange takes place in the lungs. Find out how the gas exchange takes place in creatures without lungs, such as earthworms.

Survivors

PROBLEM

How does color protect insects from predators?

Materials

yardstick (meterstick)
4 pencils
at least 82 feet (24.6 m) of string
scissors
eight 12-inch (30-cm) chenille craft stems:
    1 each of red, green, brown, black,
    white, orange, yellow, plus any other
    color you choose (These are commonly
    called pipe cleaners.)
timer
helper

Procedure

1. Find a large outdoor area with short grass. Measure a square with 20-foot (6-m) sides. Place a pencil at each corner of the square.

2. Tie one end of the string to one of the pencils. Loop the string around each of the 3 remaining pencils, and tie the free end to the first pencil to form a marked-off plot of grass.

3. Cut twenty-four ½-inch (1.25-cm) pieces of each color of pipe cleaner.

4. Without letting your helper see, spread the pieces as evenly as possible in the marked-off plot of grass.

5. Using the timer, instruct your helper to pick up as many of the pieces as possible in 1 minute.

6. Count and record the number of each color found.

7. Knowing that there should be 24 pieces of each color, calculate the number of each color not found.

Results

Your helper found some colors more easily than others and probably did not find all of the pieces.

Why?

It is hard for your helper to find colors that blend in with the grass or soil. If the grass is the same shade of green as the colored pieces, your helper will have trouble distinguishing between the two. Some of the darker-colored pieces may blend in with the shadows of the grass or with the soil.

Insects with colors that blend in with their background are said to be camouflaged. **Camouflage** is color and/or patterns that conceal an object by matching its surroundings. Camouflage protects insects from their predators (animals that kill and eat other animals). For example, a bird that feeds on grasshoppers will have trouble spotting a green grasshopper on green grass.

In this activity, your helper represents a predator, and the colored pieces found represent the different insects the predator would eat. Coloring that helps to camouflage insects from predators is called **protective coloration.**

LET'S EXPLORE

1. How does the number of predators affect the survival rate of insects? Scatter the found pieces in the plot. Repeat the activity twice, first using five helpers, then ten.

2. How does the color of the background affect which insects survive? Repeat the original experiment, using a plot of ground, half of which is not grass. **Science Fair Hint:** Take photos of the procedure and display the results.

SHOW TIME!

Model the effect of protective coloration by preparing colored pieces of bread to represent differently colored insects. Peel off and discard the crust of 4 slices of white bread. Break each bread slice into 80 small pieces. Leave the pieces of 1 slice white, but color the others red, yellow, and green. For each color, mix together ¼ cup (63 ml) of tap water and 10 drops of food coloring in a bowl. Soak the pieces of bread in the colored water, drain, then spread them out on separate trays. Allow them to air dry.

Choose an area with short grass where birds are often seen. Place 20 bread pieces from each of the 4 different colors on the grass. Spread each group in a circle of about 12 inches (30 cm) in diameter. Space the circles about 6 feet (1.8 m) apart.

Leave the area for 4 hours, then return and count the number of pieces of each color that have not been eaten. Subtract this number from 20 to determine the number of pieces eaten for each color. Repeat this procedure three times on 3 different days. Calculate the average number of pieces of each color eaten during the four trials by adding the totals for each color and dividing that total by 4.

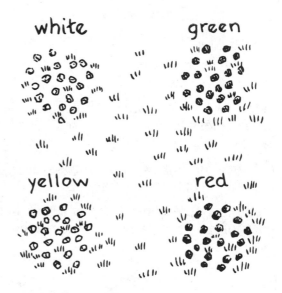

CHECK IT OUT!

Some moths have markings on their wings that look like huge eyes. These markings can frighten away predators and are a form of protective coloration called *warning coloration*. Find out more about different types of protective coloration and examples of each. What is mimicry?

Spotted

PROBLEM

How is water transported from the roots throughout plants?

Materials

2 drinking glasses
tap water
red food coloring
celery bunch with leaves
paper towels
magnifying lens
adult helper

Procedure

1. Fill each glass one-fourth full with water.

2. In one glass, add enough red food coloring to turn the water bright red.

3. Select two stalks from the innermost part of the celery bunch. They should have leaves and a pale green color.

4. Ask an adult helper to cut across the bottom of each celery stalk.

5. Stand the cut end of one celery stalk in the glass of red water, and the other in the clear water.

6. Leave the celery stalks in the glasses overnight.

7. Remove the stalks of celery from the glasses, and dry each stalk with a paper towel.

8. Use the magnifying lens to study the entire outer surface of each celery stalk.

9. Ask your adult helper to cut a 2-inch (5-cm) section from the bottom of each stalk.

10. Use the magnifying lens to study the cut surfaces of each section.

11. Ask your adult helper to cut a 2-inch (5-cm) section from each stalk at the end nearest the leaves.

12. Again, use the magnifying lens to study the cut surfaces of the celery sections.

Results

The leaves and stalk of the celery standing in the clear water are green. The stalk taken from the red water has reddish-colored leaves, and tiny red stripes run down its entire

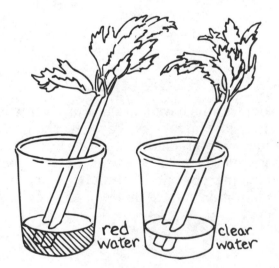

red water   clear water

length beneath the surface. Sections cut from both stalks have a single row of tiny dots near one outer edge. These dots are red in the section cut from the stalk that was in the red water. The surfaces of the cross sections cut at the top and the bottom of the same stalk are similar.

Why?

The cross sections of the celery stalk revealed that the colored water rose from the bottom of the stalk through tiny tubelike structures to the top of the stalk. These tubes, called **xylem tubes,** transport **sap** (liquid in plants) containing water and minerals from the roots throughout the plant. The red food coloring stains the thick walls of the xylem tubes, so they appear as red circles on the cross sections.

LET'S EXPLORE

1. For a closer look at the xylem tubes, ask an adult to cut a very thin slice from each stalk of celery. Place the slices on separate microscope slides and observe them under a microscope. **Science Fair Hint:** Make drawings of each slide as seen through the microscope and use them as part of a project display.

2. Do flower stems contain xylem tubes? Repeat the original experiment using a white carnation. **Science Fair Hint:** Make colored diagrams of the results of the experiment and use them as part of a project display.

SHOW TIME!

Are xylem tubes connected to one another? With the help of an adult, cut the stem of a white carnation lengthwise about halfway up the stem. Carefully separate the two halves, placing one in a glass of blue-colored water and the other in a glass of red-colored water. Observe the color of the flower after 48 hours. Study slices of the flower's stem under a microscope or magnifying lens. Photographs of the flower petals before and after the experiment can be used as part of a project display.

CHECK IT OUT!

Plants can be identified by how their xylem tubes are organized. For methods of using xylem tubes to identify plants, see pages 104–105 in Robert L. Bonnet's *Botany: 49 Science Fair Projects* (Blue Ridge Summit, PA: TAB Books, 1989).

18

Jerky

PROBLEM

How are water fleas collected and what do they look like?

Materials

wire clothes hanger
scissors
knee-high stocking
sewing needle
sewing thread
baby-food jar with lid
rubber band
paper towel
magnifying lens
adult helper

Procedure

1. Ask your adult helper to bend the hanger to form a 4-inch (10-cm) loop at one end, as shown in the diagram.

2. Use the scissors to cut the toe out of the stocking.

3. Open the cut end of the stocking and place the wire loop inside.

4. Fold the top of the stocking over the edge of the wire loop, and stitch around the fold with the needle and thread to secure the stocking to the wire.

5. Stretch the other end of the stocking over the mouth of the baby-food jar and secure it with the rubber band.

6. Have your adult helper select a place along the bank of a pond. Choose a spot with some plant growth in the water along the shore.

7. Ask your adult helper to place the jar and wire loop into the water. Then, while holding the end of the wire, move the loop toward plants growing in the water. The jar will be pulled through the water.

8. When the jar is full of water, allow excess water to drain out of the stocking before moving away from the pond.

9. Remove the rubber band and lift the stocking off the jar.

10. Place the lid on the jar and dry the outside of the jar with the paper towel.

11. Close one eye and hold the magnifying lens near your open eye.

12. With the other hand, hold the jar in front of the lens.

13. Move the jar back and forth in order to see its contents clearly. Slowly turn your body in different directions to find the best light source.

14. Study the contents of the jar and look for a tiny organism that moves through the

water with a jerky movement. If you do not see this organism, collect another sample.

NOTE: Return the water and contents of the jar to the pond. Wash your hands after working with pond water.

Results

Every sample will produce slightly different results. Varying types of plant and animal life can be collected; thus, the descriptions will vary from sample to sample and from pond to pond.

Why?

One common pond creature is daphnia, an organism about ¹⁄₁₀ inch (.25 cm) long that is visible with the naked eye and moves with a jerk. Daphnia are often called "water fleas" because they appear to jump through the water. The feathered antennae of the daphnia serve as oars, and propel the organism through the water in a series of jerky movements.

LET'S EXPLORE

1. For a closer look at the organisms in the pond water, prepare a microscopic slide following these steps:

- Place a few strands pulled from a cotton ball in the center of the slide.

- Insert an eyedropper into the water, placing the tip as close to the organisms as possible. Draw the organism, along with some water, into the eyedropper.

- Hold the eyedropper upright for 5 or more seconds to allow organisms to sink to the tip of the eyedropper. Then, squirt a drop of material onto the cotton strands and place a coverslip over the drop.

- Move the slide around slowly, observing the specimens under low power. For the best view, reduce the light on the slide.

2. Do all ponds contain the same water organisms? Repeat the original experiment, collecting specimens from different ponds. You might take your collecting net on vacation too. **Science Fair Hint:** Take photographs of the ponds and display them with diagrams of the organisms viewed in the water samples.

SHOW TIME!

Are different organisms seen at different depths in the pond? With adult assistance, use the collecting net and jar to collect samples from the surface and the bottom of the water along the bank. Prepare microscope slides from each water sample. Make sure you include any debris. Study the slide under low power, moving it around to observe all areas. Prepare diagrams of the organisms found in each sample.

CHECK IT OUT!

While daphnia is a common pond water organism, there are many others. What are the names of the other organisms seen in your pond water? For information, see pages 92–93 in *Janice VanCleave's Microscopes and Magnifying Lenses* (New York: Wiley, 1993).

Earth Science

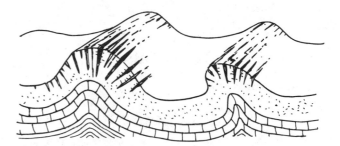

Hurricane in Northern Hemisphere

wind direction

eye

wind direction

water honey shampoo

Easy Over

PROBLEM

What happens when layers of rock are squeezed together?

Materials

4 hand towels

Procedure

1. Stack the outstretched towels on a table.

2. Place your hands on opposite ends of the towels.

3. Slowly push the ends of the towels about 4 inches (10 cm) toward the center.

4. Observe the shape of the towels.

Results

The towels form folds.

Why?

Pushing from opposite directions causes the towels to be squeezed into shapes called folds. The result is a surface with a wavelike appearance. Forces pushing toward each other from opposite directions are called **compression forces.** Such forces within the Earth can crush rocks like a mighty nutcracker, and can slowly squeeze rock layers into folds like those of the stack of towels. If the compression force is applied quickly, the rocks break, producing **earthquakes** (violent shaking of the Earth caused by a sudden movement of rock beneath its surface).

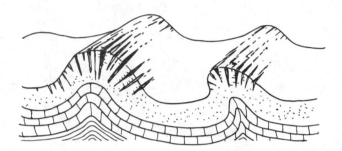

LET'S EXPLORE

1. Does the amount of force affect the results? Repeat the experiment twice, first pushing your hands *less* than 4 inches (10 cm) toward the center, and then pushing them *more* than 4 inches (10 cm) toward the center. **Science Fair Hint:** Photographs and/or diagrams showing the difference in the results can be used as part of a project display.

2. Would the type of material being compressed affect the possibility of causing an earthquake? Repeat the original experiment, replacing the towels with materials such as the following:

   • A sheet of newspaper covered with a thin layer of sand

   • A sheet of newspaper covered with a thin layer of modeling clay

Science Fair Hint: Photographs of the covered papers before and after compression can be displayed. Indicate which type of material would most likely break under pressure and thus produce earthquakes.

SHOW TIME!

1. Demonstrate how compression force crushes different materials. Cover a table with a sheet of newspaper. Place a testing material between the palms of your hands. Hold your hands over the newspaper so that any falling particles land on it. Push your hands together as hard and as fast as possible, making an effort to crush the material. Observe each material tested and describe the results. Test these items:

- A slice of bread
- A cracker
- A cookie
- An empty ice cream cone

2. Demonstrate how compression forces create folds by pushing on both ends of a large sponge. Use this as part of an oral demonstration. Diagrams of the results can be displayed.

CHECK IT OUT!

A *mountain* is a rock mass rising more than 2,000 feet (610 m) above the surrounding land. The Appalachians, the Rockies, the Himalayas, and the Alps are all examples of folded mountain ranges that were formed by compression forces. Read about folded mountain ranges, including any evidence of earthquakes in these regions.

Fiery Interior

PROBLEM

How can you make a model of Earth's interior?

Materials

2 sheets of white poster board, each
    22 × 28 inches (55 × 70 cm)
marking pen
yardstick (meterstick)
scissors
red crayon
masking tape

Procedure

1. On one sheet of the poster board, use the pen and measuring stick to draw a thermometer and the pie-shaped sections of the Earth's interior layers, using the measurements shown in the diagram.

2. Cut out the 22-by-4-inch (55-by-10-cm) section that is above the thermometer bulb from the poster board.

3. From the second sheet of poster board, cut two strips: one 14 × 28 inches (35 × 70 cm), and the second 8 × 28 inches (20 × 70 cm).

4. Use the crayon to color one whole side of the narrower strip red.

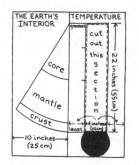

5. Cut a 10-inch (25-cm) slit 4 inches (10 cm) from the short edge of the wider strip. The slit should be centered horizontally.

6. Tape this strip behind the cut-out section of the thermometer.

7. Insert the narrow paper strip into the slit so that the red side shows through the cut-out section of the thermometer.

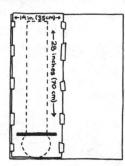

8. Tape the poster to a door.

9. Slowly pull the red strip down, and observe its height at each layer of the Earth's interior.

Results

Moving the red-colored strip up and down makes the temperature on the thermometer appear to increase and decrease. The temperature goes up as you near the core of the Earth, and goes down as you move toward the outer layers.

Why?

The Earth can be divided into three main sections: the **crust** (the outermost and coolest layer), the **mantle** (the second layer; hotter than the crust), and the **core** (the innermost and hottest layer). As the depth toward the center of the Earth increases, so does the temperature. Scientists know that the Earth's interior is hot because they find hot materials escaping through the surface from below. The temperature of the crust increases by about 86 degrees Fahrenheit (30° C) for every 0.6 miles (1 km) beneath the surface. The cause of the heat is still being investigated, but three possibilities are original heat, radioactive decay, and friction between great masses of rock. The original heat is the remainder of some of the heat trapped inside the Earth when the Earth was formed. **Radioactive decay** is the breaking apart of the **nucleus** (center) of an atom. **Friction** is the resistance to motion between two surfaces that are touching each other. Because radioactive decay and friction produce heat, there is an ongoing heating of the Earth's interior.

LET'S EXPLORE

The layers of the Earth vary in size and temperature. Use an Earth science text to determine the thickness of each layer and the temperature at the top and bottom of each layer. Add this information to the model of the Earth. **Science Fair Hint:** Display the model as part of your project.

SHOW TIME!

1. Scientists gain information about Earth's interior by studying its outer layer, the crust. Miners have discovered that high temperatures and great pressures prevent them from drilling at depths greater than about 5 miles (8 km). The molten rock that boils out of **volcanoes** (openings in the Earth's crust from which molten rock pours) gives evidence of the makeup and temperature of the inner mantle layer. Gather these and other examples of how we know about the interior of the Earth, and construct a graph with temperature on the vertical scale (bottom to top) and depth on the horizontal scale (left to right).

2. The core of the Earth has two layers: the inner core and the outer core. Find out more about the core and the other layers of the Earth's interior. Make a clay model of the Earth, using four different-colored layers of clay to represent the different layers of the Earth. Cut away a quarter section to reveal the layers. Include at least one volcano by making a small lump in the crust and showing the movement of magma from the Earth's interior to the surface. Display the model along with a key to indicate which color of clay represents each layer of the Earth.

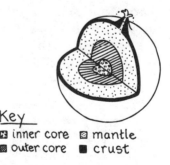

Key
◪ inner core   ▣ mantle
▨ outer core   ■ crust

CHECK IT OUT!

Most of the Earth is not visible from the surface. Use an earth science text to discover how seismic waves are used as probes to study the unseen parts of the Earth's interior. To learn more about how seismic waves are used to discover information about the Earth's structure, see *Janice VanCleave's Earthquakes* (New York: Wiley, 1993).

Combined

PROBLEM

What is the difference between rocks and minerals?

Materials

3 toothpicks
6 red gumdrops (or any dark color, such as green or black)
3 white gumdrops (or any light color, such as pink or yellow)
marking pen
3 resealable plastic bags

Procedure

1. Insert 1 toothpick each in 3 of the red gumdrops.

2. Place a white gumdrop on the other end of each toothpick.

3. Label the plastic bags Mineral 1, Mineral 2, and Rock.

4. Place 2 of the remaining red gumdrops in the bag labeled Mineral 1, and 2 of the red-and-white gumdrop sets in the bag labeled Mineral 2. In the bag labeled Rock, place the last red gumdrop and the third red-and-white gumdrop set.

Results

You have made models of two different minerals and one rock.

Why?

Rocks and minerals have two things in common. First, like all materials in the universe, they are matter. Matter is anything that has **mass** (an amount of material) and takes up space. The building units of matter are called **atoms.** If matter is made of only one kind of atom, it is called an **element.** When two or more elements are combined, the combination of elements is called a **chemical compound.** The smallest part of a chemical compound that retains the properties of the compound is called a molecule. Molecules consist of two or more atoms held together by **bonds** (connections between atoms). Second, rocks and minerals are **solids** (phase of matter with a definite shape and a definite volume).

In the experiment, the red gumdrops represent atoms of the same element, called element 1, and the white gumdrops represent atoms of a second element called element 2. The red-and-white gumdrop sets represent molecules of a chemical compound formed by the combination of atoms of element 1 and element 2. The toothpicks represent the bonds that hold atoms of the two elements together.

A **mineral** is a single solid element or chemical compound found in the Earth and that has four basic characteristics. First, a mineral occurs naturally. Rubies formed in the Earth are minerals, while man-made rubies are not. Second, a mineral is **inorganic** (not formed from the remains of living organisms). Diamonds are formed from pure carbon inside the Earth, but coal is formed from carbon that was once part of living things. Thus, diamonds are minerals, while coal is not. Third, each kind of mineral has a definite chemical composition, meaning the amount and kind of matter are the same for a given mineral. Fourth, each mineral has a definite structure known as a **crystal** (a solid made up of atoms arranged in an orderly, regular pattern). Perfect crystals have flat sides. Table salt is a mineral with crystals shaped like tiny cubes. The bag labeled Mineral 1 is a model of a mineral made up of element 1 atoms only. Mineral 2 is a model of a mineral made of molecules of atoms of elements 1 and 2.

Rocks are solids made up of one or more minerals, but they are not restricted to all four characteristics that describe minerals. The difference between rocks and minerals can be compared to the difference between model airplanes and the materials used to build them. Just as the building blocks of rocks are minerals, the building blocks of model airplanes are wheels, wings, propellers, and other parts. The main identifying characteristic of rocks is that they are mixtures. The model of the rock in this experiment is a mixture of an element and a chemical compound. Some rocks are granite, marble, and lava.

Rocks and minerals are the building blocks of the Earth's lithosphere. The **lithosphere** includes all of the Earth's crust and the upper part of the Earth's inner layer called the mantle. The lithosphere extends to a depth of about 63 miles (100 km). Thousands of different minerals have been identified in the Earth's lithosphere. Only about 12 minerals are abundant and are called **rock formers** because they make up the bulk of the lithosphere.

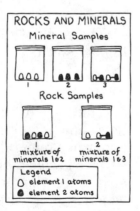

LET'S EXPLORE

Could other rocks and minerals be formed using only two types of elements? Repeat the experiment, increasing the number of red and white gumdrops as needed. Remember that minerals contain the same element or chemical compound repeated throughout, while

rocks are mixtures of different minerals. **Science Fair Hint:** Construct a display with samples of each rock and mineral model.

SHOW TIME!

Ice, which is frozen water, meets all the requirements for a mineral, but water itself does not. The symbol for water is H_2O, which means that each molecule of water is made up of two hydrogen (H) atoms connected to one oxygen (O) atom. Water exists as a solid, **liquid** (phase of matter with a definite volume but no definite shape), or a **gas** (phase of matter with no definite volume or shape). In liquid water, the oxygen atom of one water molecule loosely bonds with the hydrogen atom of another water molecule. A small flexible chain of molecules is formed. In the gas phase, fewer water molecules bond together. Ice differs from water in the liquid or gas phase in that ice is a solid with a crystalline form. The solid ice crystal is made up of water molecules, but they are bonded to form a six-sided honeycomb structure as shown in the diagram. Use gumdrops to make a model of the mineral ice. Display the gumdrop model.

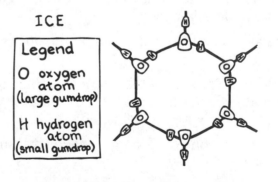

CHECK IT OUT!

Find out more about the minerals in the Earth's lithosphere. What are the names of the rock-forming minerals? For information, see pages 803–804 in Charles Wesley Chesterman's *National Audubon Society Field Guide to North American Rocks and Minerals* (New York: Knopf, 1979).

Snap!

PROBLEM

How do minerals break apart?

Materials

2 tablespoons (30 ml) plaster of paris
½ teaspoon (2.5 ml) white school glue
3-ounce (90-ml) paper cup
7 craft sticks or tongue depressors
2 teaspoons (10 ml) tap water
newspaper
timer

Procedure

NOTE: Mix the plaster in a throwaway container. Do not wash the container or the mixing stick in the sink, because the plaster can clog the drain.

1. Place the plaster and glue in the paper cup. Use one of the craft sticks as a mixing stick to thoroughly mix the glue and plaster.

2. Add the water to the cup. Mix thoroughly with the mixing stick.

3. Lay one of the craft sticks on the open newspaper.

4. Use the mixing stick to spread a thin layer of the plaster mixture over the surface of the stick lying on the paper.

5. Lay a second stick on top of the layer of plaster.

6. Repeat steps 4 and 5 to make a stack of 6 sticks with plaster between each stick.

7. Allow the plaster to dry for 1 hour.

8. Hold the stack of sticks in your hands with your thumbs on the sticks that are at the top and bottom of the stack.

9. Try to pry the stack of sticks apart by pushing with your thumbs.

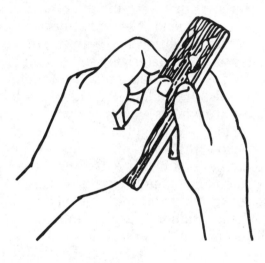

Results

The stack of sticks snaps apart, forming thinner stacks.

Why?

The stack of sticks is a model that shows how some minerals break apart. The tendency of a mineral to break along a smooth surface is called **cleavage.** A mineral may split along what is called a **cleavage plane,** which is often parallel with the face, or flat surface, of the mineral. Whether a mineral cleaves or not is determined by the arrangement of its chemical particles, such as atoms and molecules. In minerals with chemical particles that are strongly bonded, cleavage is difficult or does not occur at all. The weaker the bond between the particles, the more easily the mineral cleaves. Cleavage is one of the properties used in identifying minerals.

In the model, the sticks do not break when you push on them. Thus, the sticks represent areas of a mineral where the chemical particles are tightly held together. The surfaces of each stick are weakly bonded to the adjoining stick with plaster and glue, and these surfaces easily split apart when pressure is applied. These layers of plaster represent the areas of a mineral where chemical particles are weakly bonded. Thus, the model's cleavage planes are the areas between each stick.

LET'S EXPLORE

1. Produce models with greater and lesser cleavage. Repeat the experiment twice, first using 1 teaspoon (5 ml) glue, then using no glue. The results of these experiments represent the ease of cleavage in minerals with strong and weak bonds between chemical particles along a cleavage plane.

2. Make a model with more than one cleavage direction. Repeat steps 1 through 6 in the original experiment twice to produce two stacks of sticks. Spread a layer of the plaster-glue mixture along one of the longer sides of one of the stacks. Stand the two stacks side by side with the plaster layer between the two stacks. Gently press the two stacks together, then allow to dry. **Science Fair Hint:** As part of an oral presentation of your science project, demonstrate and explain that the model can cleave in two directions because the cleavage planes are perpendicular to each other.

SHOW TIME!

1. Demonstrate the difference between cleavage and **fracture** (uneven breaking) by tearing a paper towel in half from different directions. Most brands of paper towels tear evenly from one edge, but unevenly from an adjacent edge. Try to quickly tear a paper towel from top to bottom. Try to tear another paper towel from side to side. Photographs of the results can be used to compare cleavage and fracture.

2. Collect and display minerals having different types of cleavage.

CHECK IT OUT!

1. Use a rock and mineral handbook to find out more about cleavage. Cleavage is described as perfect, distinct, indistinct, or none. Use the handbook to determine the type of cleavage for each mineral in your display.

2. Fracture does not relate to any particular plane or direction. However, minerals that fracture do have a tendency to break apart in a certain way. Find out more about fracture. What are the different common fracture terms, and what does each type of fracture look like? Can a mineral that cleaves also fracture? Do rocks cleave and/or fracture? Add fracture type to the information card for each mineral in your display.

Changed

PROBLEM

How does oxygen weather a rock?

Materials

cup
tap water
rubber gloves
lemon-size steel wool pad without soap
 (found at stores that carry painting
 supplies)
saucer
clear plastic drinking glass

Procedure

CAUTION: Steel wool can splinter. Wear rubber gloves when handling steel wool.

1. Half-fill the cup with water.

2. Put on the rubber gloves.

3. Dip the steel wool pad into the cup of water. Hold the steel wool above the cup and allow the excess water to drain into the cup.

4. Place the moistened steel wool on the saucer.

5. Invert the glass and stand it in the saucer so that it covers all of the steel wool.

6. Place the saucer where it will not be disturbed for 3 days.

7. Each day for 5 days, put on the rubber gloves, pick up the steel wool, and rub the wool between your fingers.

Results

Each day, more of the steel wool turns reddish brown and crumbles when touched.

Why?

In the presence of water, oxygen in the air combines with the iron in the steel wool pad to form iron oxide, commonly called **rust.** The rust weakens the structure of the steel wool, causing it to fall apart when touched. Since humidity speeds up the rusting process, the glass in this experiment is used to hold moist air around the steel wool.

The chemical process in which oxygen combines with other substances is called **oxidation.** When oxygen combines with materials in rocks, the compounds formed, such as rust, weaken the structure of the rocks, making them more likely to weather.

Rocks that contain iron often have yellow, orange, or reddish brown colors. Moist air combines with the iron at the surface of these rocks to form iron oxide, and the rocks eventually crumble away as did the steel wool. The breaking down of rock into smaller pieces by natural processes is called **weathering.** The breaking down of rock by a change in its chemical composition, such as by oxidation, is called **chemical weathering.**

LET'S EXPLORE

1. Would the iron rust in the same time with no moisture? Repeat the experiment, but this time do not moisten the steel wool.

2. How would **acid rain** (rain with a higher than normal amount of acid) affect the rusting of iron? (**Acids** are substances that

yield positive hydrogen particles when dissolved in water.) Acid rain is caused when rain reacts with acid-forming gases from automobile exhausts and factories. Repeat the original experiment, adding ¼ cup (63 ml) of white vinegar, a mild acid, to the water. Make observations as often as possible every day for 3 days or until no further changes occur. **Science Fair Hint:** Keep a written record of observations and take photographs of each experiment to show the results as part of a project display.

SHOW TIME!

1. Water can chemically weather rock by dissolving minerals out of the rock. Demonstrate the dissolving effect of rain on rocks by placing 6 or more sugar cubes, which represent rocks, in a bowl. Place the bowl in a shallow baking pan. Ask an adult to use the point of a pencil to punch three small holes in the bottom of a paper cup, spacing the holes as far apart as possible. Hold your hand over the bottom of the cup while a helper fills it with water, which represents rain. Immediately place the cup about 12 inches (30 cm) above the sugar

cubes in the bowl. Remove your hand and observe the effect of the water on the sugar cubes.

2. Rain chemically weathers all rocks, but usually the change is very slow. Much of the weathering of statues and buildings made of rocks is chemical weathering due to acid rain. Rocks, such as marble, that contain carbonates weather quickly by acid. The acid combines with the carbonate to produce a gas. The weathering of marble by acid rain can be demonstrated by placing marble chips (found at plant nurseries) inside a glass jar. Fill the jar with white vinegar. Observe and record the effect of the acid on the rocks as often as possible for 1 to 2 days, or until no further changes are seen.

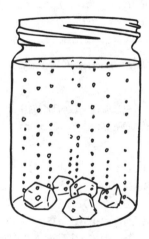

CHECK IT OUT!

Water dissolves more substances than any other liquid. Use an earth science text to find out more about chemical weathering by water. What acid is formed when carbon dioxide in air dissolves in water? What kinds of rock can this acid dissolve? How are caverns created?

Splitters

PROBLEM

How can seeds break rocks apart?

Materials

4 tablespoons (60 ml) plaster of paris
two 3-ounce (90-ml) paper cups
tap water
craft stick
4 pinto beans
marking pen
masking tape
2 paper towels

Procedure

NOTE: Mix the plaster in a throwaway container. Do not wash the container or the craft stick in the sink, because the plaster can clog the drain.

1. Place 2 tablespoons (30 ml) of plaster in each cup.

2. Add 1 tablespoon (15 ml) of water to each cup and stir with the craft stick. Discard the stick.

3. In one of the cups, stand the 4 beans as far apart as possible on the surface of the wet plaster. Push the beans into the plaster so that about three-fourths of each bean is below the surface of the plaster.

4. Use the marking pen and tape to label the cup with the beans Test and the cup without beans Control.

5. Record the appearance of the surface of the plaster in each cup.

6. Fold each paper towel in half twice. Wet the folded towels with water so that they are moist but not dripping wet.

7. Push 1 wet towel into each cup until it rests snugly against the surface of the plaster.

8. Place the cups where they will not be disturbed for a week. Wet the towels occasionally to keep them moist.

9. Remove the towels each day for 7 days and record the appearance of the surface of the plaster in each cup. Return the paper towels after each day's observation.

Results

The plaster in the Test cup cracks.

Why?

In this experiment, the plaster in the Control cup does not crack, showing you that it is the growth of the beans that causes the plaster in the Test cup to crack. As the beans grow inside the plaster, they expand, which applies pressure to the plaster. This pressure causes the plaster to crack. The same process can occur when a seed falls into a crack in a rock. The growing seed and its roots push against the rock, forcing the crack to widen and deepen. Eventually the rock can break apart. The breaking down of rock into smaller pieces by natural processes is called weathering. If the rock weathers but there is no change in the chemical composition of the rock, the process is called **physical weathering.**

LET'S EXPLORE

1. Does the size of the mock rock affect the results? Repeat the experiment twice, first using half as much plaster and water, then using twice as much plaster and water. **Science Fair Hint:** Draw diagrams daily of the surface of the plaster. Use the diagrams as part of a project display.

2. Does the amount of water on the surface of the mock rock affect the results? Repeat the original experiment twice. The first time, use dry paper towels instead of wet ones and do not add water. The second time, cover the surface of the plaster with about 1 inch (2.5 cm) of water instead of towels.

3. Do different seeds affect the results? Repeat the original experiment, using different seeds such as those of lima bean, squash, zinnia, and mustard. Test each type of seed separately. For small seeds, push the seeds into the plaster so their surface is level with that of the plaster.

4. Demonstrate the effect of plant roots that move into cracks in rocks by repeating the original experiment, but this time do not press the beans into the surface of the plaster. **Science Fair Hint:** Take photographs each day of the plaster's surface and display them along with textbook photographs of plants growing from split rocks.

5. How does the composition of the mock rock affect the results? Repeat the original experiment, replacing the plaster and water with modeling clay.

SHOW TIME!

Water that seeps into cracks in rocks and then freezes can also cause the rocks to split. This occurs because water expands as it freezes. The expanded ice acts as a wedge, widening the crack in the rock. The weathering of rock as a result of repeated freezing and thawing of water is called **frost action**. In time, frost action breaks rocks into smaller and smaller pieces. Demonstrate the expansion and force of water as it freezes by completely filling a drinking straw with water. Plug both ends of the straw with small pieces of modeling clay. Neither plug should extend past the ends of the straw. The water inside the straw should make contact with both clay plugs. Place the straw in a freezer. Observe the position of the clay plugs after 24 hours. Display a diagram showing the position of the clay plugs before and after freezing.

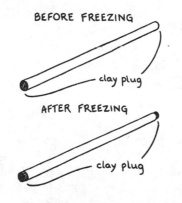

BEFORE FREEZING
clay plug

AFTER FREEZING
clay plug

CHECK IT OUT!

Physical weathering can also be caused by extreme temperature changes. Use an earth science text to find out more about physical weathering. How can burrowing animals such as earthworms, ants, and moles cause rocks to weather? What is exfoliation?

Long Enough

PROBLEM

What effect does the duration of an earthquake have on the land surface?

Materials

large shoe box
unpopped kernels of popcorn
timer
metal spoon

Procedure

1. Turn the box upside down on top of a table.

2. Cover the roof of the inverted box with a layer of popcorn kernels.

3. Hold the box steady with one hand.

4. Set the timer for 5 seconds.

5. Immediately start gently tapping the spoon on the side of the box just below the top edge.

6. Observe the movement of the kernels as you tap.

7. Stop tapping at the end of 5 seconds.

8. Set the timer for 10 seconds, and repeat the experiment.

9. Observe the movement of the kernels again as you gently tap the side of the box.

Results

Tapping the box causes the popcorn kernels to vibrate. Those kernels near the edge fall off the box, while the ones farther from the edge move only slightly. Increasing the time duration of the tapping causes more kernels to move farther away from their original position.

Why?

The longer the duration of an earthquake, the greater is the total amount of energy received by the affected area, which results in more damage. The duration of an earthquake is related to the amount of shaking energy released by the quake. Shaking energy is referred to as the **magnitude** of the earthquake and is measured by the **Richter scale** which ranges from 1 to 9. There is no absolute time of duration for earthquakes, but, generally, quakes with moderate shaking energy (magnitude up to 6) last from 5 to 10 seconds. Major quakes (magnitude of 6.5 to 7.5) last 15 to 30 seconds, while great quakes (magnitude of 7.75 or more) last for 30 to 60 seconds.

LET'S EXPLORE

1. Gentle tapping for 5 to 10 seconds represents the magnitude and duration of a moderate earthquake. Represent a major earthquake by repeating the experiment twice, first tapping harder for 15 seconds, and then tapping even harder for 30 seconds. **Science Fair Hint:** Compare the

number of popcorn kernels that fall off the box with the different magnitudes and time durations.

2. How would a different ground cover be affected by the vibrations? Cover the box with dirt, and repeat the experiment. (Perform the experiment outside, or use a tray to collect falling dirt.) **Science Fair Hint:** Pictures of the surface of the box before and after tapping on the box's side can be used as part of a science fair display. Label each diagram with the time in order of least to greatest duration.

SHOW TIME!

How are structures affected by the duration of an earthquake? Use dominoes or wooden blocks to construct "houses" about 12 inches (30 cm) from the edge of a table. Use your fist to gently hit the table nearest the houses for 10 seconds. Observe any change in the structures of the houses. Repair any damage to the houses, and then repeat by hitting the table with the same force for 30 seconds. Use photographs of the houses, before and after vibrating the table, as part of your project display.

CHECK IT OUT!

Earthquakes usually last for a short duration of from 10 to 60 seconds. Read about different recorded earthquakes, and make a chart dividing them into categories of great, major, and moderate quakes.

26 Side-to-Side

PROBLEM

How do buildings respond to lateral (side-to-side) movements produced by earthquakes?

Materials

1 sheet of coarse (rough) sandpaper
Slinky™

Procedure

1. Place the sandpaper on a table.

2. Stand the Slinky on end on the sandpaper.

3. Grab the edge of the sandpaper with your fingers, and quickly pull the paper forward about 6 inches (15 cm).

4. Observe the movement of the Slinky.

Results

The bottom of the Slinky is pulled to the side. The top section of the Slinky temporarily lags behind, and then springs back into place.

Why?

The bottom of the coil is pulled to the side by the movement of the paper beneath it. A similar movement occurs during an earthquake, when the ground below a building moves **laterally** (sideways). These lateral movements are very destructive, since they cause the walls to bend to one side. **Inertia** (the tendency of an object at rest to remain at rest) holds the upper part of the coil or a building in a leaning position for a fraction of a second, and then the structures snap back into their original shapes. During a typical

earthquake lasting only 15 seconds, a building may bend and snap between 15 and 100 times, depending on its structure.

LET'S EXPLORE

1. Earthquakes do not wait for one wave of energy to make a complete ground-to-roof-to-ground cycle before the next wave of energy enters the building. What would happen if the Slinky received energy waves from different directions? Repeat the experiment, but jerk the paper back and forth. **Science Fair Hint:** Use diagrams and/or photographs along with a written description of the results as part of a science fair project.

2. Would a taller building be more affected? Repeat the experiment, using a longer coil (connect two Slinkys). **Science Fair Hint:** Tape a paper representation of a skyscraper to the Slinky. Display the model

and photographs or diagrams indicating the changes to the building during and after the seismic (earthquake) tremors.

SHOW TIME!

Demonstrate inertia by placing the end of a 2-by-12-inch (5-by-30-cm) strip of wax paper under a glass of water. Hold the free end of the strip in your hand, and pull the paper out from under the glass with a quick, straight, forceful movement. *NOTE: This may take a little practice, so be sure to place the glass about 6 inches (15 cm) from the edge of the table to prevent it from falling off. If you pull too slowly, the glass moves forward.*

CHECK IT OUT!

Find out more about the erratic movement of structures such as buildings or bridges during an earthquake.

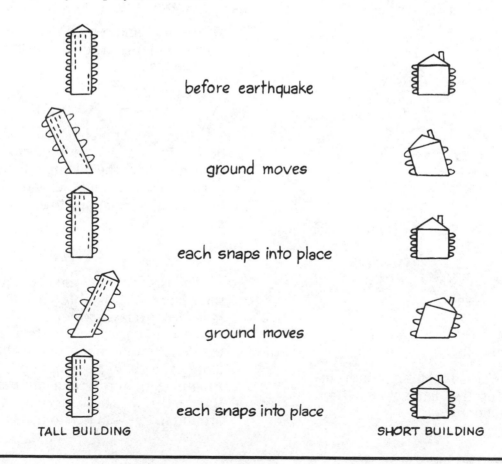

before earthquake

ground moves

each snaps into place

ground moves

each snaps into place

TALL BUILDING

SHORT BUILDING

Riser

PROBLEM

How does density affect the movement of magma?

Materials

tap water
quart (liter) jar with lid
red food coloring
spoon
1 cup (250 ml) vegetable oil
timer

Procedure

1. Pour the water into the jar.

2. Add 10 drops of the food coloring and stir.

3. Slowly add the oil.

4. Secure the lid.

5. Hold the jar so that the light from a window or desk lamp shines through the liquid in the jar.

6. Slowly turn the jar until it is upside down, and then return it to its original position.

7. Observe and record the movement of the contents inside the jar for about 30 seconds.

Results

When you first pour the oil into the jar, it floats on top of the colored water. After you tip the jar, most of the oil immediately rises again to rest above the colored water, and small bubbles of oil continue to rise for a short period of time.

Why?

The separation of the two liquids is due to their being **immiscible,** meaning they do not mix. Water has a greater **density** (measure of how much mass is in a certain volume). So, the denser water sinks to the bottom and the less dense oil floats to the top. Like the oil, **magma** (liquid rock beneath the surface of the Earth), which is less dense than the rock around it, tends to rise to the surface. Magma begins its upward movement from depths of 35 to 50 miles (56 to 80 km) beneath the Earth's crust. This upward journey can be caused by pressures within the Earth, but more often magma rises because its density is lower than that of surrounding material.

LET'S EXPLORE

Does shaking the bottle longer affect the results? Repeat the original experiment, shaking the jar vigorously for 5 seconds. Record your observations every 5 minutes for 30 minutes, and then continue checking every hour until no further changes occur. Shaking the oil and water can be used to simulate mixing magma with denser materials. How does mixing the materials affect the material of lesser density? **Science Fair Hint:** Diagrams showing the contents of the jar at different time intervals can be made and used as part of a project display.

SHOW TIME!

1. Unless restricted by pressure, hot materials **expand** (get larger) and cold materials contract (get smaller). All rock materials do not expand at the same rate; thus, within the Earth some of the heated rocks expand and become less dense than the surrounding rock material. You can demonstrate the difference in the densities of a compressed material and the same material when it is expanded. To do so, roll a lemon-size piece of clay into a ball. Then, shape another similar-size piece of clay into an open box; be sure to make the box as large as possible. Place both pieces of clay on the surface of a container of water.

2. To demonstrate the way one material will rise through another due to differences in density, fill a plastic dishwashing liquid bottle halfway with vegetable oil and secure the lid. Fill a small aquarium with water. Add a few drops of blue food coloring to the water and stir, making the water lightly colored. Turn the dishwashing liquid bottle on its side and push it down to the bottom of the aquarium. Open the spout and gently squeeze the bottle. Use photographs of the experiment as part of a project display.

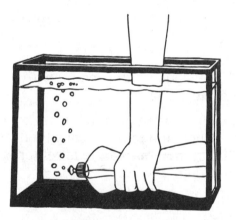

CHECK IT OUT!

At times it appears that magma moves through solid rock. By a process called *stoping,* blocks of solid rock in the path of magma are broken, melted, and added to the flowing hot, liquid rock. Use an earth science text to find out more about magma. Does magma always reach the Earth's surface? Learn about the effects that the movement of magma has on the Earth's crust, such as the production of earthquakes.

28 Magma Flow

PROBLEM

How does temperature affect the movement of magma?

Materials

teaspoon (5-ml spoon)
soft margarine
small baby-food jar
cereal bowl
warm tap water
timer

Procedure

1. Fill the teaspoon (5-ml spoon) with margarine.

2. Using your finger, push the margarine out of the spoon and into the baby-food jar so that the glob of margarine is centered in the bottom of the jar.

3. Hold the jar in your hand and turn it on its side.

4. Observe any movement of the margarine.

5. Fill the bowl halfway with warm (slightly hotter than room temperature) tap water.

6. Set the baby-food jar in the warm water.

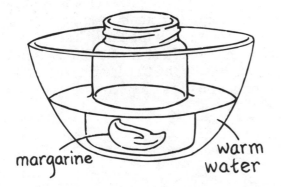

margarine   warm water

7. After 3 minutes, pick up the jar and turn it on its side.

8. Again, observe any movement made by the glob of margarine.

Results

At first the margarine inside the tilted jar does not move much, but heating the margarine causes it to move more freely.

Why?

As the temperature of the margarine increased, it became thinner and moved more easily. Molecules (smallest part of a substance that keeps the properties of that substance) in colder materials have less energy, are closer together, and move more slowly than warmer molecules with more energy. These warm, energized molecules move away from each other, causing solids to melt and liquids to thin. Just as the temperature of the margarine affected the way it moved across the surface of the jar, the temperature of magma affects the way it moves up the volcano's **vent** (the channel of a volcano that connects the source of magma to the volcano's opening). Hot magma is thin and moves easily and quickly up the vent, while cooler magma is thick and sluggish.

LET'S EXPLORE

1. Would a different heating time affect the results? Repeat the experiment, checking

the movement of the margarine every minute for 6 minutes. Use a thermometer to keep the temperature of the water as constant as possible, and replace the warm water each time you make an observation. Quickly replace the jar in the warm water after each testing.

2. Does the composition of the material being heated affect the results? Repeat the original experiment, using other solids such as butter or chocolate candy with and without nuts.

SHOW TIME!

1. Thick liquids are said to have a high **viscosity** (the measurement of a liquid's ability to flow). Viscous liquids flow slowly, and particles dropped into the liquid fall slowly as well. Liquids such as water, honey, and shampoo can be used to simulate magma of various viscosities. Test the viscosity of each liquid by dropping a marble into a tall, slender glass filled with the liquid at room temperature. The slower the marble falls, the more viscous the liquid is.

2. Demonstrate the effect of temperature on the viscosity of the liquids by repeating the

previous experiment twice. First, raise the temperature of the samples by standing each glass in a jar of warm water. After 3 minutes, stir the liquids and use a thermometer to determine the temperature of each. Second, lower the temperature of the samples to about 50 degrees Fahrenheit (10° C) by inserting a thermometer in each liquid sample and placing them in a refrigerator. Diagrams and the results of each experiment can be used as part of a project display.

CHECK IT OUT!

The three distinct types of magma—*andesitic, basaltic,* and *rhyolitic*—harden into different kinds of rock. Find out more about the characteristics of these magma types. What is their chemical composition? Where are they formed? How does the temperature of each differ? Which is the most common? For information about magma, see pages 74–79 in *The Dynamic Earth,* Second Edition (New York: Wiley, 1992), by Brian J. Skinner and Stephen C. Porter.

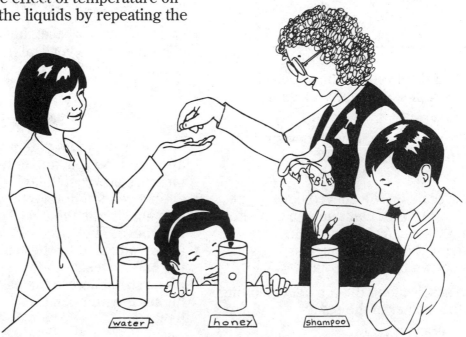

Windy

PROBLEM

How can the speed of wind be measured?

Materials

drawing compass
poster board square, 6 × 6 inches
   (15 × 15 cm)
scissors
ruler
marking pen
transparent tape
12-inch (30-cm) piece of thread
Ping-Pong ball

Procedure

1. Use the compass to draw a curved line connecting two diagonal corners of the piece of poster board as shown in the diagram.

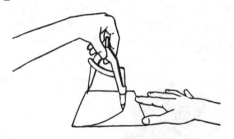

2. Cut along the curved line and keep the cone-shaped piece of paper. Discard the rest.

3. Lay the paper on a table with one straight edge at the top and the other straight edge to the right.

4. Prepare a scale on the curved edge of the paper by using the ruler and pen to make nine evenly spaced sections along the curved edge. Number them, starting with zero, as shown in the diagram.

5. Draw an arrow along the top edge pointing toward the corner of the paper.

6. Turn the ruler over and tape the paper to the top edge of the ruler as shown.

7. Tape one end of the thread to the Ping-Pong ball.

8. Tape the other end of the thread near the corner of the paper. The thread should hang so that it crosses the zero mark on the paper.

9. Stand outside in a windy area. Hold the ruler and point the arrow in the direction from which the wind is blowing.

10. Observe where the string crosses the paper scale.

Results

In a gentle breeze, the string moves slightly from its vertical position. A faster breeze causes the string to move farther up the scale.

Why?

The instrument you built is called an **anemometer.** An anemometer is used to measure how fast the **wind** (movement of air in a general horizontal direction) blows. Moving air hits the Ping-Pong ball and causes it to move. The speed of the wind hitting the ball is indicated by the scale number to which the ball moves, as determined by the position of the string across the paper scale. The higher the number, the faster the wind is blowing.

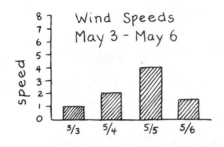

Wind Speeds
May 3 - May 6

speed: 8 7 6 5 4 3 2 1 0

5/3   5/4   5/5   5/6

LET'S EXPLORE

Use the anemometer you just made to measure the wind speed each day for a week or more. Record your readings in a data chart. **Science Fair Hint:** Use the information from the data chart to construct a graph similar to the graph shown here. Display the chart, graph, and anemometer as part of a project display.

SHOW TIME!

1. Construct another type of anemometer called a Robinson anemometer by crossing two drinking straws and taping them together in the center where they cross. Use a pencil to punch a hole in the side of a 3-ounce (90-ml) paper cup near its rim. Do the same to three other cups that size. Place a cup on the end of each straw and secure with tape. All of the cups must face in the same direction. Ask an adult to stick a straight pin through the center of the straws and into the eraser of a pencil. Move the straws back and forth to enlarge the hole made by the pin so that the straws rotate easily around the pin. Hold the pencil upright and position the cups about 12 inches (30 cm) from your face. Blow toward the open end of the cups to make sure the cups will spin around in a breeze. Use the cups to make comparisons of wind speeds on different days. The speed of the wind hitting the cups is determined by the number of turns per minute made by the cups. The faster the wind, the more turns per minute. Use this anemometer to determine wind speed (number of turns per

minute) over several days. Compare your results with predicted wind speed from daily weather reports in the newspaper and/or on local television. Display the anemometer and the collected results.

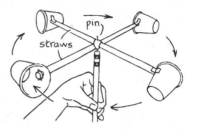

pin
straws

2. You can figure out the wind's direction simply by observing which way tree limbs, shrubs, or grass are blowing and then using a compass to determine what direction that is.

3. A **weather vane** (instrument that shows wind direction) can be constructed by marking the directions, N, NE, E, SE, S, SW, W, and NW along the rim of a paper plate. Place the plate on the ground in an unobstructed area. Attach a 4-inch (10-cm) piece of string to the top of a pencil eraser with a piece of tape. Insert the point of the pencil through the center of the paper plate and about 1 inch (2.5 cm) into the ground. Use a compass to determine which way is north, and rotate the paper plate until the N marked on the plate points north. The string will blow in the same direction as the wind. Photographs of the weather vane can be displayed.

CHECK IT OUT!

The *Beaufort Scale* is one in which human observations are used to determine the speed of the wind. For example, smoke rising straight up from a chimney indicates a wind speed of less than 1 mile (1.6 km) per hour. What are other Beaufort Scale examples? For information, see pages 96–97 in Spencer Christian's *Can It Really Rain Frogs?* (New York: Wiley, 1997).

Stormy

PROBLEM

What is the eye of a hurricane?

Materials

2-quart (2-liter) plastic bowl
tap water
scissors
string
ruler (the kind that has been punched for a
    three-ring binder)
paper clip
masking tape
black pepper
wooden spoon with a long handle

Procedure

1. Fill the plastic bowl three-fourths full with water.

2. Cut the string so that it is 1 inch (2.5 cm) longer than the height of the plastic bowl.

3. Tie one end of the string to the paper clip.

4. Thread about 1 inch (2.5 cm) of the free end of the string through the hole in the center of the ruler. Tape the end to the ruler.

5. Sprinkle pepper over the surface of the water in the bowl.

6. Stir the water with the spoon in a counterclockwise direction a few times.

7. While the water is swirling, quickly suspend the paper clip in the center of the swirling water. Try to drop the paper clip directly in the center of the spiral made by the swirling pepper specks.

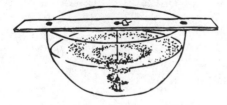

Results

As long as the paper clip remains in the exact center of the swirling water, it moves slightly or not at all.

Why?

The swirling water in the experiment represents a **hurricane.** A hurricane is a large tropical storm with winds of 74 miles (118 km) per hour or more that rotate around a relatively calm center. The center of the swirling water in this experiment simulates the calm area in the center of a hurricane called the eye of a hurricane. The eye is a long, vertical tube of relatively motionless air in the middle of the storm. The distance across the eye of a hurricane varies depending on the size of the storm, but it averages about 20 miles (32 km) across. This area of calm air reaches all the way to the Earth's surface and has high-speed winds spinning around it. In the Northern Hemisphere a hurricane's winds spin counterclockwise around the eye, and in the Southern Hemisphere the winds spin clockwise. Like the air in a hurricane's eye, the area in the center of the swirling water in the bowl is relatively calm, as is indicated by the paper clip's lack of motion.

LET'S EXPLORE

1. How would suspending the paper clip near the side of the bowl affect the results? Repeat the experiment twice, first suspending the paper clip in the water on the side nearest to you, and then suspending the paper clip in the water on the side farthest from you. **Science Fair Hint:** Use the results of this experiment to illustrate how the direction of the winds of a hurricane would change as it passed directly over you. Find out more about the weather conditions you would experience during a

hurricane. A diagram illustrating the results can be used as part of a project display.

Hurricane in Northern Hemisphere

wind direction

eye

wind direction

2. Does the size of the container affect the results? Repeat the experiment twice, first using a smaller bowl, and then using a larger bowl. **Science Fair Hint:** Find out more about the size of hurricane eyes. Does the size of the eye increase as the storm increases? Does the rotation speed of the storm affect the size of the hurricane's eye? Display drawings of hurricanes, comparing their size to the size of their eyes.

SHOW TIME!

1. Where is the rotation speed of swirling water the fastest? Fill a 2-quart (2-liter) bowl three-fourths full with water. Place a piece of tape on the top edge of the bowl. Cut two small triangles from a piece of notebook paper. Slowly stir the water in a circular motion. Drop one of the paper triangles near the center of the water. At the same time, ask a helper to drop the second paper triangle in the water near, but not touching, the side of the bowl. Count the number of times that each piece of paper passes the tape in 10 seconds. (Hint: You should each keep track of one triangle.)

You should repeat this experiment at least three times and calculate the average number of rotations for each piece of paper. How do your results relate to the difference in the speed of winds of a hurricane near its eye and the speed of winds at its outer edges?

2. The official hurricane season for North Atlantic hurricanes is June 1 through November 30. Find out the dates for the hurricane season in your area, request a hurricane tracking map from your local media weather station, and plot the positions of hurricanes. For information about plotting the coordinates of a hurricane, see pages 116–123 of *Janice VanCleave's Geography for Every Kid* (New York: Wiley, 1993).

CHECK IT OUT!

1. Hurricanes occur on every continent except Antarctica. In Australia they are called *willy-willies*. Find out more about the different names given to hurricanes in various parts of the world. Make and display a map of the world showing hurricanes with their special names.

2. Hurricanes almost always begin over tropical seas during late summer and early fall. Moist air and heat are the two fuels needed to start and maintain these storms. Find out more about the birth and growth of these storms. What water-surface temperature is needed? What are the names of the different stages of development, and what is the wind speed of each stage? Which way do hurricanes move? What is their traveling speed? What is the average life span of hurricanes?

Wash Out

PROBLEM

How do slow, low-energy waves affect a beach?

Materials

paint-roller pan
1 quart (1 liter) sand
2 quarts (2 liters) tap water
pencil

Procedure

1. Cover the bottom of the pan with the sand, building up a small "beach" at the shallow end.

2. Pour the water into the deep end of the pan.

3. Make a mental note of the appearance of the sandy beach in the pan.

4. Make waves by laying the pencil in the deep end of the pan and slowly moving the pencil up and down with your fingertips. Push the pencil about 1 inch (2.5 cm) below the water each time.

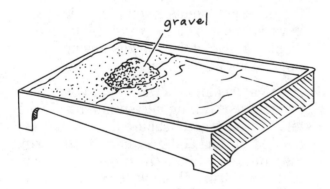
gravel

5. Observe the beach after the water waves have hit against it.

Results

The water washes some of the sand from the "beach" and moves it to the deeper part of the pan.

Why?

The area where the ocean and the land meet is called the **shoreline.** The **shore** is the land at the shoreline. If it is a smooth, sloping stretch of sand and pebbles, the shore is called a **beach. Water waves** are repeating disturbances on the surface of water. When ocean waves hit the beach, water moves forward for a short distance, then drains back toward the deeper part of the pan. As the water drains, some of the sand moves with the water. Along a real shoreline, the waves bring sand toward the beach in one area as they strip sand away from another area. This **displacement** (movement from one place to the other) of sand is an example of **erosion.** In this experiment, the slow, low-energy waves erode away a small part of the beach.

LET'S EXPLORE

1. How would fast, high-energy waves affect the results? Repeat the experiment, quickly moving the pencil up and down, pushing the pencil at least 2 inches (5 cm) below the water each time. **Science Fair Hint:** Make a diagram similar to the one here showing the sea, the shoreline, and the beach.

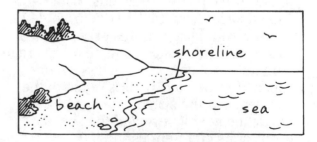
shoreline
beach
sea

2. How does the material on the shore affect the results? Repeat the original experiment, using aquarium gravel instead of sand.

SHOW TIME!

1. Weathering is the process by which rocks are broken into small pieces. One type of weathering is called **abrasion,** which occurs when rocks rub against each other and wear each other down. Demonstrate abrasion. First, observe the surface of a large rock; then, rub a piece of coarse sandpaper against the rock's surface. Again observe the rock's surface.

2. **Currents** (swift streams of water) in oceans flow parallel to the shoreline. This moving water transports **sediments** (weathered rock material). When the water is slowed, it deposits some of the sediment it is carrying. Demonstrate how the movement of water affects the amount of sediment it deposits. Fill a jar about half full with tap water. Add ¼ cup (63 ml) of sand, and close the jar with its lid. Holding the ends of the jar, turn it sideways and hold it at eye level. Shake the jar vigorously ten or more times observing its contents. Notice any sand buildup on the lower side of the jar. Repeat, shaking the jar gently.

CHECK IT OUT!

Headlands are projections of land that extend from the shore into deep water. These projections slow incoming waves and deflect them away from the beach. Find out more about headlands. How do waves affect headlands? How are sea cliffs formed from headlands? How are sea caves, sea arches, and sea stacks formed? Diagrams of the progression of the erosion of headlands into other rock structures can be displayed. For information, see pages 87–94 in *Janice VanCleave's Oceans for Every Kid* (New York: Wiley, 1996).

Floaters

PROBLEM

How can you model the position of an iceberg in water?

Materials

3-ounce (90-ml) paper cup
tap water
timer
wide-mouthed quart (liter) jar
2 teaspoons (10 ml) table salt
spoon
NOTE: This project requires a freezer.

Procedure

1. Fill the cup with water.

2. Place the cup in the freezer for 2 hours or until the water in the cup is completely frozen.

3. Fill the jar three-fourths full with water.

4. Add the salt to the water in the jar and stir.

5. Remove the ice from the cup. To do this, wrap your hands around the cup for 5 to 6 seconds. The warmth from your hands melts some of the ice, making it easy to remove.

6. Tilt the jar and slowly slide the ice into the jar.

7. Observe the amount of ice above and below the surface of the water.

Results

More ice is below the water's surface than above it.

Why?

When water freezes, it expands. The density of ice is slightly less than the density of water. As a result, ice floats in water, but is only slightly lifted above the water's surface. The greater the difference between the density of water and the density of ice, the higher the ice floats in the water. **Icebergs** (large mass of floating ice in the ocean), like the ice in this experiment, float in seawater, which is salty. Icebergs would float slightly lower in freshwater because the difference in density between ice and freshwater is less than that between ice and seawater.

LET'S EXPLORE

Arctic icebergs are generally jagged pieces of ice. How does this irregular shape affect the position of the iceberg in the water? Repeat the experiment, making two cups of ice. Remove the ice from the cups, and place the two pieces on a plate. Wet 2 to 3 ice cubes with water and stack them on one of the blocks of ice. Put the plate back in the freezer for 10 minutes. Place the ice pieces into a large see-through bowl filled about three-fourths full with water. Compare the amount of ice each block has above and below the water's surface.

SHOW TIME!

1. Antarctic icebergs are **tabular** (table top) in shape. Make a model of a tabular iceberg by forming a rectangular mold from a 12-by-18-inch (30-by-45-cm) piece of heavy-duty aluminum foil. Make a shallow box out of the piece of foil by following these steps:

   - Fold the foil in half three times to make a 4½-by-6-inch (11.25-by-15-cm) rectangle.

   - Fold up about 1 inch (2.5 cm) on each edge of the foil rectangle to make the sides of the box.

   - Fold each corner of the foil to one side so that it is snug against the sides of the box.

   Fill the foil box with water and set it on a plate. Place the plate in the freezer for 3 hours, or until the water in the box is completely frozen. Fill a 2-quart (2-liter) transparent bowl three-fourths full with water; add 1 tablespoon (15 ml) of table salt and stir. Remove the ice from the foil box by peeling away the foil. Place the ice in the bowl, and observe the amount of ice above and below the surface of the water.

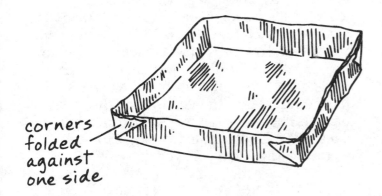

corners folded against one side

2a. The color of the ice in icebergs depends on the materials trapped inside the ice and how compressed the ice is. Trapped air bubbles tend to reflect more light, causing the ice to look milky white. Design a way to freeze water with different amounts of air bubbles. The warmer the water, the less gas dissolved in it. Try freezing both warm and cold water. Fill one 3-ounce (90-ml) paper cup with warm water and a second cup with cold water. After the water freezes, compare the color of the two ice samples.

b. Another possible way to increase the amount of air bubbles might be to mix the water with air. Repeat the previous experiment, but pour the cold water into a jar. Seal the jar and shake it vigorously to mix the water and air inside. Then, pour the water into the paper cup for freezing. Again, compare the color of the frozen samples. For more information about the color of icebergs, see pages 158–159 in *Janice VanCleave's Oceans for Every Kid* (New York: Wiley, 1996).

CHECK IT OUT!

Some Arctic icebergs are as large as a 10-story building. But not all bergs are king-size; some are small. Those measuring up to about 33 feet (10 m) across are called *growlers*. Find out more about icebergs. What are bergy bits? How does the size of Arctic and Antarctic icebergs compare? How are icebergs formed? Where are most of the icebergs formed? For information, see ice and ice formation in an encyclopedia.

Indicators

PROBLEM

How do scientists gather clues to climates of the past?

Materials

modeling clay in three different colors
2 index cards
1 teaspoon (5 ml) rice
drinking straw
fingernail scissors
magnifying lens
adult helper

Procedure

1. Soften the clay by squeezing it in your hands. Break off a walnut-size piece of each color of clay.

2. Flatten one of the clay pieces, and lay it in the center of one index card.

3. Sprinkle the rice over the top surface of the flattened clay piece.

4. Flatten the remaining two pieces of clay and stack them on top of the layer of rice. A three-layer block of clay about 1 inch (2.5 cm) deep will be formed.

5. Push the straw through the layers of clay.

6. Pull the straw out of the clay.

7. Ask your adult helper to use the scissors to cut open the straw.

8. Carefully remove the clay plug and lay it on the second index card.

9. Use the magnifying lens to study the clay plug.

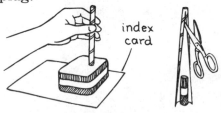

index card

Results

The straw cuts a cylinder-shaped sample with three layers of clay and possibly some visible rice.

Why?

As the straw cuts through the clay, the clay and rice are pushed up inside the hollow tube. The clay represents different layers of the Earth's crust, and the rice represents solids, such as **fossils** (traces of the remains of pre-historic organisms). The captured clay is called a **core sample,** and it reveals what materials are inside the block of clay. Machines called coring devices are used to cut through layers of soil just as the straw cuts through the layers of clay. The coring device has a plunger that pushes the soil out so that materials at different depths below the Earth's surface can be studied.

Scientists use core samples taken from ocean floors to discover important clues about the **climate** (average weather in a region over a long period of time) in past times. **(Weather** is the result of changing conditions in the layer of air surrounding Earth called the atmosphere.) These samples contain tiny ocean creatures known as **foraminifera,** which are about one-fifth as wide as a human hair. These creatures have been preserved in the ocean floor for millions of years, and their shells have different shapes and makeups depending on the climate in which they were formed. These core samples give scientists clues of the Earth's major climate changes over the last million years or more.

LET'S EXPLORE

1. Is the clay block exactly the same through-out? Repeat the experiment, cutting core samples with the straw from different parts of the clay block. **Science Fair**

Hint: Use diagrams to represent the size, shape, and color of each layer in the core samples.

2. The rice may not be visible on the outside of the core, but slices of the core sample can provide a better view of the core's content. Construct a saw to cut slices from the core sample by tying each end of a 4-inch (10-cm) sewing thread to toothpicks with rounded ends. Pull the toothpicks apart so that the thread is straight and taut between them. Place the thread on top of the core sample near one end. Move the toothpicks back and forth to saw a slice from the end of the clay. Use the magnifying lens to study the surface of the slice of clay.
Science Fair Hint: Display photographs of core samples and slices along with diagrams of the magnified surfaces of the samples.

SHOW TIME!

1a. Trees can give clues to the weather of the past. The growth rings of trees reveal good and bad growing seasons of past years. Contact your local parks department or a tree-trimming company and request a slice from a tree trunk or limb to be used as part of your science display. Find out more about the growth rings of trees. How do the rings indicate the age of the tree? What differences appear in growth rings during good and bad growing seasons? Display the tree slice, and label rings from these good and bad seasons. Note the age of the tree from which the slice was taken.

b. Examine the slice and use a pictograph similar to the diagram to represent the good and bad growing seasons during the life of the tree.

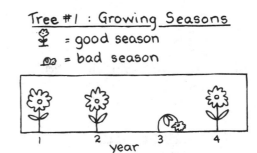

c. If possible, collect different tree slices and compare growth seasons during the same years. Prepare a pictograph of growing seasons for each tree slice.

d. If one is available, use a measuring instrument called calipers to more accurately determine the width of the growth rings in a cross section of a tree branch or trunk. Compare the width of each ring to the average rainfall and temperature during the year that the ring was formed. Ask a local media meteorologist for information about the average rainfall and temperature in the area where the tree grew.

CHECK IT OUT!

Core samples taken in ice layers contain bubbles of air. These tiny trapped air bubbles show which gases were present in the atmosphere when falling snow trapped the air. Find out more about other clues left by nature that reveal information about past climates. How are fossil plants, pollen, and animals used as past climate indicators? How do rocks give clues to the presence and size of glaciers?

How Old?

PROBLEM

How can you model a method for dating fossilized bones?

Materials

hand towel
masking tape
marking pen
bowl
small empty coffee can with a lid
100 pennies
timer

Procedure

1. Stretch the towel out on a table.

2. Use the tape and marking pen to label the bowl Changed and the can Unchanged.

3. Place all of the coins in the can.

4. Set the timer for 1 minute.

5. At the end of 1 minute, pour the coins out of the can and onto the towel. (The towel keeps the coins from rolling off the table.)

6. Transfer half of the coins to the bowl. Record this as being the first division.

7. Return the remaining coins on the towel to the can.

8. Again, set the timer for 1 minute.

9. Continue to separate the coins at the end of each minute, keeping track of how many divisions are made. Stop when the number of coins is so small that you cannot divide it (when only one coin remains in the can). Record this as being the last division. *NOTE: When trying to divide odd numbers, such as 25 coins, place the closest even number back into the can. For 25 coins, return 12 coins to the can.*

10. Count the number of divisions made.

Results

The coins are divided seven times.

Why?

Elements that are **radioactive** have undergone radioactive decay. In this experiment, each 1-minute division of the coins represents one **half-life** (the time it takes for one half of the mass of a radioactive element to decay). At the end of 1 minute, half of the coins were placed in the bowl (changed) to demonstrate the change that occurs in radioactive elements, such as those found in fossilized bones. After another minute, half of the remaining coins were placed in the bowl, leaving only one-fourth, or 25 coins, in the can (unchanged) and a total of 75 coins in the bowl. As time passed, the number of coins in the bowl increased, but the number of coins in the can decreased, just as all radioactive elements will eventually change. The half-life for this experiment was 1 minute. While some half-lives are less than this, many are thousands, millions, and even billions of years.

The amount of original radioactive material is determined and compared to the amount of unchanged radioactive material in a **fossilized** (hardened trace of an organism from past geologic times) bone to determine its age. The original amount of radioactive material in a dinosaur bone is estimated by comparing the bone to that of a bone of a similar animal living today. The amount of original radioactive material left in a dinosaur bone indicates the age of the bone.

LET'S EXPLORE

1. How does the half-life time affect the number of divisions? Repeat the experiment dividing the coins every 2 minutes.

2. How does the mass affect the number of divisions? Repeat the original experiment using 50 coins.

SHOW TIME!

1. Another way that scientists date fossilized bones is by determining their relative age. The **relative age** of an object or event is its age as compared with that of another object or event. Finding the relative age simply places things in order of occurrence. In a group of rock layers, each layer is usually younger than the one beneath it and older than the one above it (except when the Earth has been moved through natural or man-made events).

Model the way that deposited sediments form rock layers over a period of time. Using ½ cup (125 ml) each of three different colors of aquarium gravel, pour one color of gravel into each of three bowls. Add ½ cup (125 ml) of soil or sand to each bowl of gravel. Stir. Fill a 2-quart (2-liter) rectangular glass baking dish halfway with water. Use your hand to sprinkle the gravel-soil mixture from one of the bowls into the water. Wait 10 minutes and observe the appearance of the layer

formed by the mixture. Sprinkle the gravel-soil mixture from one of the remaining bowls into the water. Again, wait 10 minutes and observe the appearance of the materials in the dish. Add the last gravel-soil mixture. After 10 minutes, observe the contents of the dish.

2. A drawing of the layers formed in the previous activity can be compared to fossils found in three time periods, such as Cretaceous, Jurassic, and Triassic. Design a diagram with a legend showing dinosaur fossils found in these three time periods such as the one shown here.

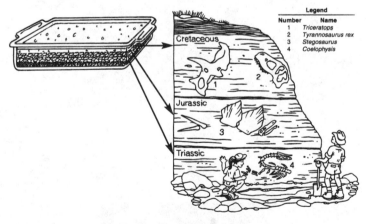

CHECK IT OUT!

The dinosaur era is known as the Mesozoic era and is divided into three parts called the Triassic, Jurassic, and Cretaceous periods. How old are each of the time periods? How do these time periods fit into the Earth's geologic timescale? For information, see pages 41–49 in *Janice VanCleave's Dinosaurs for Every Kid* (New York: Wiley, 1994).

Engineering

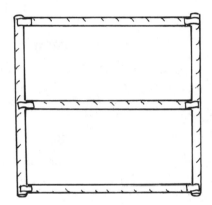

LATERAL BRACE

Flexible

PROBLEM

How do earthquakes affect unbraced frame structures?

Materials

masking tape
4 drinking straws
sheet of office paper
marking pen
helper

Procedure

1. Tape 4 straws together to form the outline of a square form.

2. Lay the sheet of office paper on a table.

3. Position the straw frame on the lower right-hand corner of the paper.

4. Use the marking pen to draw around the outside of the square frame.

5. Hold the bottom straw firmly against the paper with your left hand.

6. Use your right hand to push the top straw as far to the left as possible without breaking the frame.

7. Hold the frame in this leaning position while a helper marks around the outside of the frame.

Results

The bottom of the frame stays in place while the top and sides lean toward the left. The top of the frame can be as much as 2 inches (5 cm) to the left of the original positon.

Why?

The straw, as well as the tape joining the straws together, allows the structure to be **flexible** (able to bend without breaking). Frame structures with **vertical** (up-and-down) supports allow the most flexibility and movement, which can be dangerous to the occupants and damaging to the furnishings of the swaying building. The lateral (sideways) movement of a building during an earthquake can bend the structure's frame to a point that it breaks, causing the structure to collapse.

LET'S EXPLORE

1. Would a **lateral brace** increase the strength of the building and reduce the deforming flexibility? Repeat the experiment, placing a straw horizontally across the center of the frame.

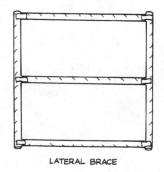

LATERAL BRACE

2. How would a solid wall affect the strength and deforming flexibility of the structure? Solid walls connected to a frame are called **shear-wall bracings.** To test their effect, repeat the experiment while covering the

original square frame with a piece of cardboard. Use tape to secure the cardboard to the frame. **Science Fair Hint:** As part of a project, display the shear-wall bracing model, as well as models representing a vertical- and a lateral-braced frame. Include diagrams indicating the amount of flexibility of each structure.

SHOW TIME!

Buildings in earthquake areas that survive earthquakes must be able to bend without breaking. Test the flexibility of different strips of building material by securing each strip to an outdoor table with a C-clamp. (NOTE: If you use an indoor table, place a rug or towels beneath the pail.) Add weights to the end of the strip by placing rocks in a pail attached to the end of the strip. Continue to add the rocks to the pail until the pail is full or the strip cracks. Display the various materials tested with a comparison of their flexibility.

CHECK IT OUT!

In choosing a metal support for a building, the elasticity and tensile strength of the metal must be considered. Define *tensile strength* and *elasticity,* and explain why they are especially important when selecting building supplies in earthquake areas.

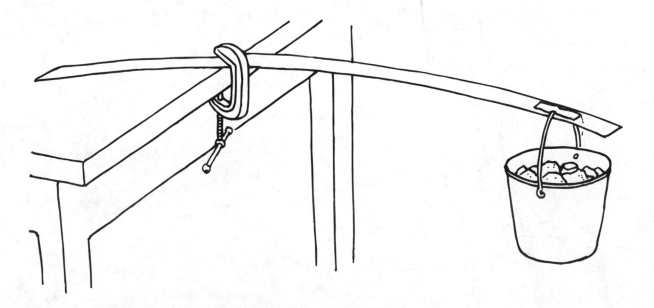

Windmill

PROBLEM

How can a model of a windmill be made?

Materials

scissors
ruler
sheet of office paper
pencil
large coin (quarter)
paper hole-punch
drinking straw
modeling clay
sewing thread
paper clip

Procedure

1. Cut a 6-by-6-inch (15-by-15-cm) square from the sheet of paper.

2. Draw two diagonal lines across the paper square so that you have an X.

3. Use the coin to draw a circle in the center of the square.

4. With the hole-punch, make one hole in each corner of the square as indicated in the diagram.

5. Make a hole through the center of the circle with the point of the pencil.

6. Cut the four diagonal lines up to the edge of the circle in the center.

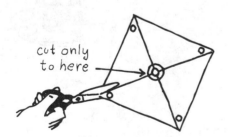

cut only to here

7. To form a paper wheel-of-sails, fold the corners with the holes over the center,

one at a time, aligning all the holes with the hole in the center of the paper.

8. Push a drinking straw through the holes, and position the paper wheel in the center of the straw.

9. Wrap a small piece of clay around both sides of the straw next to the paper wheel to keep the wheel in place.

10. Cut a 2-foot (60-cm) piece of sewing thread.

11. Tie one end of the thread about 2 inches (5 cm) from one end of the straw.

12. Tie the free end of the thread to the paper clip.

13. Hold your hands upright in front of your face, with your thumbs pointing toward your body.

14. Cradle the ends of the straw in the grooves formed between your index fingers and thumbs. Do not grip the straw.

15. Blow toward the paper windmill.

16. Observe the movement of the paper wheel, straw, and paper clip.

Results

The paper wheel and the straw turn. The string attached to the straw winds around the turning straw, and thus the paper clip rises.

Why?

Machines are devices that make work easier. The paper wheel and the straw form a simple machine called a **wheel and axle** (a large wheel to which a smaller wheel or axle is attached). Connecting the thread and paper clip produces a model demonstrating how a windmill works. The paper sails of the model windmill act as a wheel and turn in a large circle; the straw is the axle and turns in a smaller circle. The wheel and axle turn together, but the wheel makes a bigger circle than the axle does. As the wheel makes one large turn, the string winds once around the turning axle; the load (the paper clip) rises a distance equal to the distance around the axle. It takes less force to raise the load (the paper clip) by turning the larger wheel than by lifting the load with your hands. (A **load** is the object moved by a machine.)

LET'S EXPLORE

1. Does the size of the wheel affect the results? Repeat the experiment twice, each time changing the size of the paper wheel. First construct a wheel using a 3-by-3-inch (7.5-by-7.5-cm) square, and then construct a wheel using a 12-by-12-inch (30-by-30-cm) square.

2. Would a different-size axle affect the results? Repeat the original experiment, using a knitting needle for a smaller axle. Repeat again, using a dowel rod with a circumference larger than that of the straw.

SHOW TIME!

Construct a model of a waterwheel, which is another example of a wheel-and-axle machine. Ask an adult to cut the top off a 2-liter plastic soda bottle, and cut two notches about ½ inch (1.3 cm) wide and 2 inches (5 cm) deep in the top edge of the plastic bottle directly across from each other. Cut holes in the side, toward the bottom of the bottle, to allow water to flow out. Construct a waterwheel by gluing a series of paper blades cut from index cards to the body of an empty thread spool. Push a pencil through the center of the spool. Secure the spool to the pencil with tape. Cradle the ends of the pencil in the cut-out sections at the top of the bottle. Tie one end of a string to a paper clip, and tape the free end to the pencil. Place the bottle in a sink, under a faucet. Turn on a slow trickle of water. The water should hit against the paper blades. The spool and pencil will rotate and the string will wind around the pencil, raising the paper clip. Display the model of the waterwheel as part of a project display, along with photographs taken during the experiment.

CHECK IT OUT!

The first windmill was built in Persia in the seventh century A.D. This classic example of a wheel-and-axle machine depends on the wind as its power source; thus, the sails can be turned so that they always face into the wind. Find out more about the design of windmills and how they are designed to cope with varying wind speeds. Include information about windmills of the past that contained jib and spring sails, along with modern wind turbines that drive generators instead of pumps and grindstones.

Physical Science

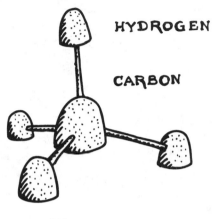

HYDROGEN

CARBON

METHANE

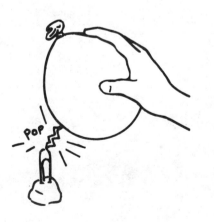

POP

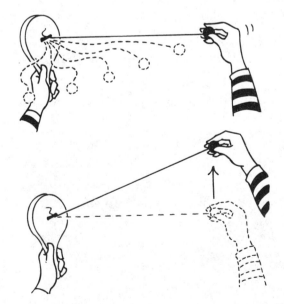

I.D.

PROBLEM

How can you test for the presence of an acid?

Materials

red cabbage
food blender
distilled water
food strainer
large bowl
1-quart (1-liter) jar with lid
masking tape
marker
white saucer
1 teaspoon (5 ml) vinegar
spoon
adult helper
NOTE: A refrigerator is required for this experiment.

Procedure

1. Make a cabbage acid indicator by following these steps:

   • Fill the blender halfway with cabbage leaves, then cover them with distilled water.

   • Ask an adult to blend the water and cabbage.

   • Ask an adult to assist in straining the contents of the blender into the bowl.

   • Pour the cabbage indicator into the jar. Label the jar Cabbage Indicator. *NOTE: Close the jar and store in the refrigerator when not in use to prevent the indicator from spoiling.*

2. Use the indicator to test for an acid by following these steps:

   • Place 2 tablespoons (30 ml) of cabbage indicator in the saucer.

   • Observe the color of the cabbage indicator.

   • Add the vinegar to the indicator. Stir.

   • Observe the color of the liquid in the saucer.

Results

The cabbage indicator changes from purple to red when mixed with vinegar.

Why?

The blender breaks open the cells of the cabbage and the colored chemicals inside the cells mix with the water. The juice that forms turns a pink-to-red color when mixed with an acid, such as vinegar. The cabbage juice is an **indicator** (a chemical that changes color in an acid and/or base).

LET'S EXPLORE

What effect do **bases** (a substance that yields a negative hydroxyl ion when dissolved in water) have on the cabbage indicator? Repeat step 2 of the experiment, placing an antacid tablet in the indicator. Allow the tablet to sit for 2 to 3 minutes, then stir.

SHOW TIME!

1. Do all materials that dissolve in water produce hydrogen or hydroxyl ions? Prepare and test the following materials using the red cabbage indicator: salt, sugar, flour, cleaning powder, Epsom salts, vinegar, lemon juice. Prepare the solids by adding 2 teaspoons (10 ml) of each solid material to 1 cup (250 ml) of distilled water. The liquid materials can be added directly to the indicator solution. No change in color indicates a **neutral solution,** one that is neither acidic nor basic. A chart of the resulting colors along with conclusions of each test can be used as part of a project display.

2. Can other dyes extracted from plants be used as indicators? Test with juices from grapes, blackberries, or other berries.

3. Find out more about acids and bases. What are some common examples of acids and bases? Prepare a display of foods representing acids and bases by using photos cut out of magazines.

CHECK IT OUT!

Acid indigestion is due to an excessive production of stomach acid. Find out what acid is produced in the stomach and what causes an excess production of acid. How do antacid tablets remove the excess stomach acid? A physician or pharmacist can provide information about this.

Super Chains

PROBLEM

*What is the physical structure of methane, the simplest **hydrocarbon** (molecule containing hydrogen and carbon atoms)?*

Materials

4 toothpicks
1 large black gumdrop
4 small white gumdrops

Procedure

1. Stick the toothpicks in the large black gumdrop. Space the toothpicks so that they are an equal distance from one another.

2. Place 1 small white gumdrop on the end of each toothpick.

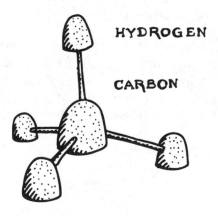

HYDROGEN

CARBON

METHANE

Results

You have made a molecular model for methane.

Why?

Hydrocarbon molecules are composed of carbon and hydrogen atoms. Each carbon atom in a hydrocarbon molecule has four bonds (connections between atoms) that are equally spaced, and each hydrogen atom has one bond. Methane is the simplest hydrocarbon molecule. In the methane structure, the single black gumdrop represents one carbon atom bonded (attached) to four hydrogen atoms represented by the white gumdrops. The chemical formula used to represent methane is CH_4. The formula, like the model you made, shows that the methane molecule has one carbon atom and four hydrogen atoms.

LET'S EXPLORE

What would be the shape of a hydrocarbon with two carbon atoms? Ethane contains two carbon atoms and six hydrogen atoms. The chemical formula for ethane is C_2H_6. To construct an ethane model, first connect two large black gumdrops with a toothpick. Then stick three toothpicks in each of the connected black gumdrops. Space the toothpicks so that all the toothpicks in each black gumdrop are an equal distance from one another. Place one small white gumdrop on the end of each toothpick. **Science Fair Hint:** Display models of methane and ethane as part of a project.

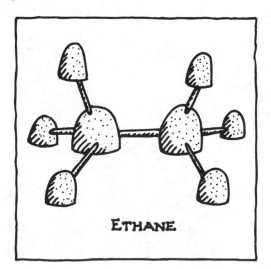

ETHANE

SHOW TIME!

1. What shapes do other hydrocarbons such as propane (C_3H_8) and butane (C_4H_{10}) have? Remember that each carbon atom in a hydrocarbon molecule has four bonds that are equally spaced, and each hydrogen atom has one bond. Display all the models constructed as part of a project display.

2. A structural formula for a hydrocarbon molecule is used to illustrate the number of connected carbon and hydrogen atoms. Complete the "Hydrocarbons" chart and display with the models of each molecule.

HYDROCARBONS		
NAME	FORMULA	STRUCTURAL FORMULA
Methane	CH_4	H H–C–H H
Ethane	C_2H_6	H H H–C–C–H H H
Propane	C_3H_8	
Butane	C_4H_{10}	

CHECK IT OUT!

Read about hydrocarbon gases such as methane, ethane, propane, and butane. Write and display a report about these gases. Include in the report answers to questions such as:

- Why is methane called marsh gas?

- Which of the gases are used as home fuels?

Stickers

PROBLEM

How is static electricity produced?

Materials

9-inch (23-cm) round balloon
ruler
scissors
sewing thread
masking tape
hand soap
water
towel
adult helper and a hair dryer if the air
   is humid

Procedure

NOTE: This experiment works best on a dry day. If the air is very humid, ask an adult to dry the balloon with a hair dryer.

1. Inflate the balloon and knot the end.

2. Tie a 12-inch (30-cm) piece of thread to the balloon.

3. Tape the free end of the string to the edge of a table.

4. Wash and dry your hands. Your hands must be clean and very dry.

5. Sit on the floor near the balloon.

6. Hold the balloon in one hand and quickly rub the other hand back and forth across the surface of the balloon eight to ten times.

7. Release the balloon and allow it to hang freely.

8. Hold the hand rubbed against the balloon near and to the side of, but not touching, the balloon.

Results

The balloon moves toward your hand.

Why?

Static electricity is energy due to the buildup of electric charges on an object. These charges are called **static charges** because they are **stationary** (not moving). These static charges can be positive or negative. All substances are made up of atoms. Every atom has a nucleus containing protons and electrons spinning around it. The **protons** have a positive electrical charge, and the **electrons** have a negative charge. When two substances such as the balloon and your hand are rubbed together, electrons are pulled over from the material that has the weaker attraction for them (the hand) and attach to the material that has the stronger attraction (the balloon). This causes both materials to become electrically charged. The material losing electrons becomes positively charged and the material gaining electrons becomes negatively charged.

The diagram shows that the balloon and hand are **electrically neutral** (containing an equal number of positive and negative charges) before rubbing—that is, each have an equal number of positive and negative charges. After rubbing, the balloon has extra negative charges and the hand is left with extra positive charges. Electric charges follow certain rules, and one rule states that unlike charges are attracted to each other; thus, the negatively charged balloon is attracted to the positively charged hand because of the difference in their charges. Notice in the diagram that there is no change in the total number of combined positive and negative charges on the objects before and after rubbing them together. The rubbing causes the already-present electrons to move from one object to the other.

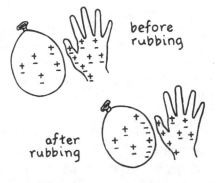

before rubbing

after rubbing

LET'S EXPLORE

1. Does the number of times the balloon is rubbed affect the results? Repeat the experiment twice: first, decrease the number of times the balloon is rubbed, and then increase the number of rubbings.

2. Would rubbing the balloon with different materials affect the results? Repeat the original experiment, rubbing the balloon with different types of cloth such as cotton, wool, silk, and/or rayon and with materials such as paper and plastic. **Science Fair Hint:** Photographs taken during the testing of the materials, the testing materials themselves, and the results of the test can be used as part of a project display.

3. Does the shape of the balloon affect the results? Repeat the original experiment,

replacing the round balloon with a long balloon and/or balloons with wavy shapes.

SHOW TIME!

1. Demonstrate that there is an excess of charge on the area where the balloon is rubbed. Use a marker to put an X on the area of the balloon to be rubbed. Repeat the original experiment, giving the balloon a slight spin to cause it to rotate. The balloon will turn and stop with the X facing your hand.

2. Another way to demonstrate static electricity is to lay about 20 pieces of puffed rice cereal on a table. Wad a 2-foot (60-cm) piece of plastic food wrap to form a piece about the size of your fist. Quickly rub the plastic wrap back and forth across a sheet of paper 10 to 15 times. Immediately hold the plastic above the puffed rice. The plastic should be near, but not touching, the cereal.

3. Clothes removed from a clothes dryer often cling to each other. Prepare a display using simple diagrams or photographs to represent common everyday examples of the effect of static electricity.

CHECK IT OUT!

Use an encyclopedia, physical science text, and/or other books about electricity to find out more about static electricity. What kind of materials are more likely to be positive? Or negative? How do static charges affect electrical equipment?

Zap!

PROBLEM

What happens when static electricity is discharged?

Materials

scissors
ruler
plastic report folder
modeling clay
large paper clip
wool scarf

Procedure

1. Cut a 2-by-8-inch (5-by-20-cm) strip from the plastic report folder.

2. Use a walnut-size piece of clay to stand the paper clip upright on a table.

3. Darken the room and wrap the scarf around the plastic strip.

4. Quickly pull the plastic through the scarf. Do this rapidly at least three times.

5. Immediately hold the plastic near, but not touching, the top of the paper clip.

Results

A bright spark of light leaps between the plastic strip and the paper clip.

Why?

Like all atoms, the atoms in the paper clip have a positive center, the nucleus, with negatively charged electrons spinning around it. Rubbing the plastic against the wool causes some electrons from the wool to collect on the plastic. This buildup of electrons produces what is called static electricity. These static charges follow the law of electric charges, which states that like charges repel each other and unlike charges attract each other. Holding the negatively charged plastic near the electrically neutral paper clip causes the negatively charged electrons in the clip to move away because of the repulsion between like charges. This creates a positive charge on the surface of the clip near the plastic.

When the charge on the plastic is great enough, the air between the two materials also becomes charged, thereby forming a path through which electrons can move. The resulting spark is called a **static discharge,** which is a loss of static electricity. This discharge can be a very slow, quiet transfer of charges or, as in this experiment, quick with a spark of light and/or a crackle of sound.

LET'S EXPLORE

1. Does the number of strokes of the wool against the plastic affect the results? Repeat the experiment twice, first rubbing the plastic once, and then rubbing the plastic six times.

2. Does the material being charged affect the results? Repeat the original experiment, replacing the plastic strip with materials such as a clean drinking glass and a rubber comb.

SHOW TIME!

1. Lightning is one of the most spectacular displays of static discharge. All of the processes that lead to separation of positive and negative charges in a cloud are not fully understood. Some processes that cause charge separation are the splitting of water drops, the freezing of water or melting of ice, and the rubbing of materials together.

   During a thunderstorm, violent air currents move up and down inside the clouds, rubbing water droplets and ice crystals against each other. This movement is but one of the processes that fills the clouds with a charge of static electricity—just as rubbing the plastic and wool together in the original experiment produced a charge.

   Find out how the discharge of static charges produces lightning between two clouds and between a cloud and the ground. Use this information to prepare a display chart of the events leading up to a flash. Include steps such as:

   • the location of charges in a cloud

   • the movement of a "stepped leader"

   • upward streams of positive charges

   • a stroke of lightning

   For more information about lightning, see pages 126–127 in *USA Today: The Weather Book,* by Jack Williams (New York: Vantage Books, 1992).

2a. Demonstrate that static discharge electricity produces **radio waves** a form of **electromagnetic radiation** (energy in the form of waves that can travel through space). This can be done by tuning an AM radio to a position between stations and setting a very low volume. Charge an inflated balloon by rubbing it quickly across a piece of wool about ten times (or rub the balloon against your clean, dry, oil-free hair). As you hold the balloon near, but not touching, the radio antenna, listen for a single pop that will be heard as the static electricity is discharged from the balloon. For more information about radio waves produced by static discharge, see page 180, "Micro-Bolt," in *Janice VanCleave's Earth Science for Every Kid* (New York: Wiley, 1991).

b. To see another example of the electromagnetic radiation, repeat the previous experiment, this time holding the charged balloon near, but not touching, a paper clip as in the diagram. This works best in a darkened room. The spark of light is a type of electromagnetic radiation.

CHECK IT OUT!

According to information found on pages 111–114 in *The Weather Companion,* by Gary Lockhart (New York: Wiley, 1988), lightning is not equally attracted to all trees. Use this book and other resources to discover which trees are more likely to be struck by lightning. What are the characteristics of trees that are more electrically attractive?

Hot Box

PROBLEM

What is the greenhouse effect?

Materials

shoebox
soil
2 thermometers
colorless plastic food wrap
timer

Procedure

1. Half fill the shoebox with soil.

2. Lay one of the thermometers on the surface of the soil. Keep the second thermometer outside of the box.

3. Cover the opening of the box with a single layer of plastic wrap.

4. Take a reading from both thermometers.

5. Place the box and second thermometer side by side in a sunny place outdoors.

6. Record readings from both thermometers every 15 minutes for one hour.

7. Record readings every hour thereafter for 4 hours.

Results

All or most all of the temperature readings show that the temperature inside the plastic-covered box was higher than the temperature outside the box.

Why?

A structure designed to provide a protected, controlled environment for raising plants indoors is called a **greenhouse.** It is made of glass or other material that allows the sun's light to pass through. The box in this experiment is an example of a greenhouse.

Solar energy is electromagnetic radiation. This energy is emitted by the Sun and comes in the form of waves of varying wavelengths. The short-wavelength radiation from the Sun passes freely through the plastic wrap covering the box. Most of this energy is absorbed by the soil and cardboard sides of the box, causing them to heat up. Long-wavelength radiation, called **infrared** radiation (heat waves), is then released by the soil and the cardboard sides.

Some scientists think that short-wavelength radiation enters the box through the plastic and changes into long-wavelength radiation, or heat waves, which are then trapped inside by the plastic. Other scientists believe that because greenhouses are closed, heated air becomes trapped inside. Since no cooling air can enter the box, the temperature inside the greenhouse increases.

The Earth's atmosphere, however, does trap the long-wavelength radiation. The composition of gases in air is about 78 percent nitrogen, 21 percent oxygen, and 1 percent water vapor, carbon dioxide, and other gases such as neon, sulfur dioxide, and carbon monoxide. Like the plastic over the box in this experiment, the atmosphere allows solar energy to pass through to the Earth's surface. The surface heats up and gives off long-wavelength radiation. Most of these heat waves are absorbed by **water vapor** (water in its gas phase) and carbon dioxide (gas produced by burning fuels and exhaled by animals) in the lower atmosphere. These atmospheric gases reemit a large portion of the heat waves back toward the Earth, which causes the Earth's surface to gradually become warmer. The greenhouse and the atmosphere both trap warmth from the Sun. For this reason, this warming of the Earth is called the **greenhouse effect.**

LET'S EXPLORE

1. Does the type of cover on the box affect the results? Repeat the original experiment, preparing boxes with different covers. One can be covered with glass. Ask an adult to remove a piece of glass from a picture frame and to place masking tape around the edges. Cover other boxes with transparent plastic report folders of various colors. **Science Fair Hint:** Display samples of the box covers with the results of the experiment.

2. Do surface structures affect the results? Repeat the original experiment, preparing several boxes. Cover the surface of the soil in the boxes with different materials, such as rocks, leaves, and grass. **Science Fair Hint:** Display photographs of the various boxes with the results of the experiment.

3. Design ways to cover the box so that you can determine if it is the lack of air circulation or the trapped heat rays that affect the temperature change.

SHOW TIME!

1. The gases in the Earth's atmosphere keep the Earth from cooling too quickly at night. Simulate the atmosphere's effect on temperature by preparing two boxes as in the original experiment, but leave one box uncovered. Put the boxes outdoors in a sunny area for 3 hours, and then place them inside the house in a dark area such as a closet. Read the thermometers every 15 minutes for 1 hour and then every 30 minutes for at least 2 hours thereafter.

2. **Ozone** is a form of oxygen that contains three combined oxygen atoms; the oxygen we breathe contains two combined oxygen atoms. The largest amount of ozone exists at a height between 10 and 20 miles (16 and 32 km) above the Earth's surface; this area of the atmosphere is called the **ozone layer.** Some scientists think that reduction of the ozone layer would allow more radiation from the Sun to reach the Earth's surface, eventually causing climate changes.

   Terrariums (closed containers housing small plants and possibly some small animals such as snails, frogs, or snakes) can be used to simulate, though not exactly, the effect of increased solar radiation. Prepare two small, identical terrariums using instructions from a nursery or a book on building terrariums. Insert a thermometer in each terrarium. Place one terrarium near a window where it will receive direct sunlight most of the day. Place the other terrarium away from direct sunlight, but in a lighted area. Observe both terrariums for at least 30 days. Take photos of the terrariums at the beginning and then on random days during the experiment. Find out more about the ozone layer and how people are causing it to change. Use this information to prepare a poster, and display it along with the terrariums.

Up and Down

PROBLEM

How can you make a model of a Fahrenheit thermometer?

Materials

2 sheets of white poster board, each
　22 × 28 inches (55 × 70 cm)
yardstick (meterstick)
scissors
red crayon
marking pen
transparent tape

Procedure

1. From one of the sheets of poster board, cut a 14-by-28-inch (35-by-70-cm) strip and an 8-by-28-inch (20-by-70-cm) strip.
2. Color the bulb on the large strip and one side of the narrower strip red.
3. On the larger strip, draw a thermometer using the measurements shown in the diagram.
4. Cut out and remove the 4-by-22-inch (10-by-55-cm) section above the thermometer bulb.
5. From the second sheet of poster board, cut a 14-by-28-inch (35-by-70-cm) strip.
6. Cut a 10-inch (25-cm) slit 4 inches (10 cm) from the short edge of the strip. The slit should be centered horizontally.
7. Place the strip behind the thermometer and tape the edges of the two strips together.
8. Insert the narrow paper strip into the slit so that the red side shows through the cut-out section of the thermometer.

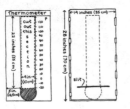

9. Holding the poster, slowly pull the red strip down and observe its height at each temperature mark.

Results

Moving the red-colored strip up and down makes the temperature reading on the thermometer increase and decrease.

Why?

A **thermometer** is an instrument used to measure temperature. **Temperature** measures how hot a material is, which equals the average **kinetic energy** (energy of motion) of the molecules in the material. The higher the temperature of a material, the faster its molecules are moving around. As molecules move faster, they move farther apart. In a real thermometer, as the material in the bulb gets hotter, it expands and moves up the tube. As the material cools, its molecules move slower and move closer together, and the material moves down the thermometer tube.

A thermometer is **calibrated.** This means that the different heights along the tube are marked so that the distance from one mark to the next represents a change of the same number of degrees in the temperature of the material.

LET'S EXPLORE

1. Use a thermometer calibrated in both Fahrenheit and Celsius to mark Celsius degrees on the model. **Science Fair Hint:** Find out more about the thermometer scales of Fahrenheit and Celsius and how they differ. Display examples of calculations showing how Fahrenheit degrees are mathematically changed to Celsius degrees and examples of Celsius degrees changed to Fahrenheit degrees.

2. Weather is the result of changing conditions in Earth's atmosphere. The study of weather is called meteorology, and the scientists who study weather are called **meteorologists.** One condition of the atmosphere that changes is its temperature.

   Meteorologists often refer to the freezing point of water (32 degrees Fahrenheit and 0 degrees Celsius) when measuring air temperature. A temperature expected to be below freezing indicates that the air temperature will drop below 32° F (0° C). Mark the freezing point of water on the thermometer model. **Science Fair Hint:** Display the model as part of your project.

SHOW TIME!

1. Another way to demonstrate how a thermometer works is by constructing a bottle thermometer. Stand a very thin drinking straw in a cup half filled with water that has been tinted with blue food coloring. While the straw is in the water, place your index finger over the open end of the straw. Keeping your finger over the straw, lift the straw out of the colored water and insert the free end into an empty soda bottle. Ask a helper to seal the mouth of the bottle by wrapping clay around the straw; then remove your finger from over the end of the straw. Fill a bowl with warm tap water. Fill a second bowl with cold tap water and add two or three ice cubes. Place the soda bottle containing the straw in the warm water. When the colored water in the straw starts to rise, remove the bottle from the water and quickly set it in the bowl of ice water. Display drawings that show the position of the colored water in the straw when the bottle thermometer is heated and cooled.

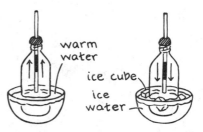

2. Sensory receptors in your skin can detect changes in temperature. See if your skin can give you accurate information about temperature. Number three bowls and fill them with water of different temperatures: bowl 1, lukewarm; bowl 2, cool; bowl 3, icy cold. Ask a helper to place a finger in bowl 1 and a second helper to place a finger in bowl 3. After 30 seconds, instruct both helpers to immediately place their fingers in bowl 2. Have them each describe the temperature of the water in bowl 2.

CHECK IT OUT!

A weather observer could not give a complete report of weather conditions without knowing the air temperature. The thermometer is thus a tool that is very important to meteorology. Find out more about the thermometer. Who invented the first thermometer? Who suggested the first thermometer scale? What kinds of thermometers did Gabriel D. Fahrenheit, Anders Celsius, and Lord Kelvin introduce? Information about thermometers can be found on pages 181–187 in *Janice VanCleave's A+ Projects in Chemistry* (New York: Wiley, 1993).

Launcher

PROBLEM

How are satellites launched into orbit around the Earth?

Materials

cardboard box
2 plastic rulers with groove down center
modeling clay
marble

Procedure

1. Turn the cardboard box upside down on top of a table.

2. Place the edge of the box 10 inches (25 cm) from the edge of the table.

3. Lay one ruler on top of the box with 4 inches (10 cm) of the ruler extending over the edge of the box.

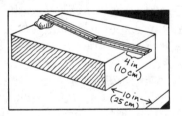

4. Hold the second ruler so that one end touches the end of the first ruler, with the grooves of the rulers lined up, and the second end is 2 inches (5 cm) above the box. Support that end by placing a piece of clay under it.

5. Position a marble at the top of the raised ruler, and then release the marble.

6. Observe the path of the marble.

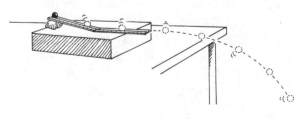

Results

The marble rolls down the ruler and off its end. The marble's path curves downward after it leaves the end of the "launcher" until it hits the floor.

Why?

The table represents the Earth, and the top of the box is a position above Earth's surface. The marble represents a satellite. A **satellite** is a body that moves in a curved path about a celestial body. The "marble satellite" is launched horizontally, parallel to the Earth's surface. All satellites are raised to a desired height above Earth by booster rockets, and then with additional rocket power the satellite is launched parallel to Earth's surface. Neither the "marble satellite" nor a space satellite continues to move forward in a straight line, because gravity pulls them toward Earth.

The marble moves in a curved path out over the tabletop and past the edge of the table because gravity pulls it down and its launching speed pushes it forward. A space satellite also moves in a curved path, but it continues to curve completely around Earth. This curved path of one body about another is called an **orbit.** The horizontal launching speed of any man-made satellite, like that of the marble, has to be great enough to balance the pull of gravity. Its forward speed, combined with the pull of gravity, keeps it away from the Earth's surface and moving in a curved path.

LET'S EXPLORE

1. If the horizontal launching speed is too slow, gravity pulls the satellites back to Earth's surface. Demonstrate this by repeating the experiment with the end of one ruler raised less than 2 inches (5 cm) above the box.

2. If the horizontal speed is too great, the craft breaks away from the Earth's gravitational pull and escapes into space. You cannot cause the marble to actually escape into space, but repeating the experiment with the raised end of the launcher higher than 2 inches (5 cm) will demonstrate the movement of the satellite away from the normal path produced in the original experiment. **Science Fair Hint:** The launcher and pictures of the launcher could be used as part of a project display.

3. Does the weight of the marble affect its speed? Follow the procedure of the experiment, but use a larger, heavier marble. Record any difference in the path of the marble.

SHOW TIME!

1. A cartoon diagram similar to the one shown may help to demonstrate the effect that launching speed has on placing satellites into orbit.

2. Multistaged rockets are used to place satellites into orbit. How is this achieved? What happens to each part of the system? Balloons and a paper cup can be used to demonstrate rocket staging. The diagram gives a clue to the construction of a multistage rocket system. A diagram of this balloon model along with pictures of actual multistaged rockets would make a good project display.

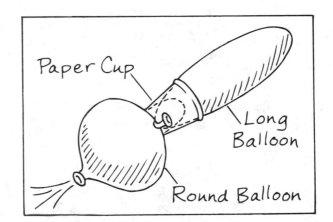

CHECK IT OUT!

1. Weather satellites stay in the same place above the Earth's surface. They are said to be in a *geosynchronous orbit*. Read about geosynchronous orbits on pages 184 and 185 of *Janice VanCleave's Astronomy for Every Kid* (New York: Wiley, 1991). Write to NASA for information about satellites. Your parent or teacher can assist you in securing the address.

2. Read about the space shuttle and how it launches satellites. What does it mean to say satellites "fall" into orbit? NASA can provide printed material about the space shuttle and satellites.

Toys and Gravity

PROBLEM

How does gravity affect playing paddle ball?

Materials

paddle ball

Procedure

1. Hold the paddle in one hand and the ball in the other hand.

2. Pull the ball straight out from the paddle as far as your outstretched arms or the elastic will allow.

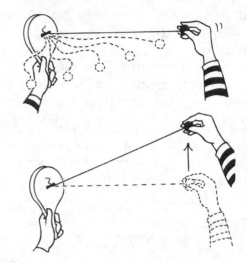

3. Release the ball.

4. Observe the path of the returning ball.

5. Again pull the ball straight out from the paddle as far as your outstretched arms or the elastic will allow. Raise the ball up about 1 foot (30 cm) from its horizontal position.

6. Release the ball and observe its path.

7. Continue to change the position of the ball until its returning path directs it to the center of the paddle.

Results

The returning ball misses the paddle when it is stretched straight out from the paddle. Holding the ball at a height higher than the top of the paddle results in the ball striking the center of the paddle.

Why?

The string pulls the ball toward the paddle, but gravity pulls the ball toward the center of the Earth, which is straight down. These two forces cause the ball to continue to fall and at the same time move toward the paddle. The result is that the ball moves in a curved path that arches downward. When pulled straight out, the ball's curved path brings it lower than the paddle's handle. The raised ball still moves in a curved path that arches down-ward, but the new path ends in the center of the paddle.

LET'S EXPLORE

How far does the ball drop before reaching the paddle? The diagram illustrates a method for determining this distance. The paddle is partially covered with black paper and the ball dipped in flour. The ball is pulled straight out from the paddle and released. A white spot on the black paper marks the point of the returning ball. **Science Fair Hint:** The paddle and paper can be attached to the project display and used to demonstrate the effect of gravity on the toy.

SHOW TIME!

1. Does gravity make a Slinky™ slink? Place the toy on the top step of "stairs" made by stacking books, and give it a slight push forward. Observe the movement and direction of the Slinky. Can it be made to climb up the steps? *(NOTE: A metal Slinky will give the best results.)* Photographs and a written description of the results can be displayed.

2. Does the height of the steps affect the movement of the Slinky? Build steps of different heights with books. Test the Slinky's movement at different heights. Display the record of each height used and the resulting movement of the toy.

3. Collect and display toys that need gravity to work. A short explanation about how each toy works with the help of gravity should accompany each toy.

CHECK IT OUT!

How would toys that depend on gravity behave in space? NASA has tested the behavior of these toys in space: paddle ball, Slinky, yo-yo, ball and jacks, flip toy, wind-up car, paper airplane. Predict and record how you think the toys might behave in space. Remember that in orbiting spacecraft, the pull of gravity is so weak that objects are virtually weightless. Then, find out how these toys actually behaved in space, and compare this data with your predictions. Your teacher can secure a videotape from NASA showing the actual testing of these toys during a space mission.

Lifter

PROBLEM

What is a first-class lever, and what is the advantage of using one?

Materials

lightweight table
sturdy chair (the back should be as tall as the table)
broom

Procedure

1. Put one hand under the edge of the table (be sure there's nothing on it) and gently push upward. Try to lift the end of the table off of the floor. *WARNING: Do not strain if the table is heavy.*

2. Place the back of the chair about 4 inches (10 cm) from the edge of the table.

3. Lay the broom handle over the back of the chair and under the edge of the table.

4. Place your hand on the straw end of the broom and gently push down.

Results

The end of the broom handle rises, lifting the table off the floor. Using the broom to raise the table takes less effort than trying to lift the table with your hand.

Why?

Machines are often thought of as complicated devices with many moving parts that are powered by a motor. Scientists define a machine as any device that changes either the direction or the amount of force that you must apply to accomplish a task. The broom acts as a kind of simple machine called a **lever.** A lever is a rigid bar that pivots around a fixed point called a **fulcrum.** There are three different kinds of levers: first-class, second-class, and third-class. One type is not superior to another; each just has the fulcrum in a different place.

The broom in this experiment is an example of a **first-class lever,** which always has the fulcrum (in this case, the chair back) between the **effort force** (the push or pull needed to move an object) and the load (the object being moved). A first-class lever changes the direction of the force; one end of the lever moves up when the other is pushed down. With this type of lever, less effort force is used when the **effort arm** (the distance from the fulcrum to the point where you apply the effort force) is longer than the **load arm** (the distance from the fulcrum to the load). Because your force was multiplied by the lever, it was easier to move the table with the lever than with your hand.

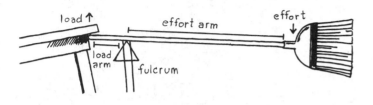

LET'S EXPLORE

1. Would the position of the fulcrum (the chair back) affect the results? Repeat the experiment, placing the chair at different distances from the edge of the table. **Science Fair Hint:** Use diagrams to represent the different positions of the fulcrum. Indicate which positions require the most and the least amount of effort to lift the table.

2. Would the length of the lever affect the results? Repeat the original experiment twice, first replacing the broom with a shorter rod, and then with a longer rod.

SHOW TIME!

1. Put one end of a pencil under a stack of books. Use a second pencil as a fulcrum by placing it under the first pencil. Push down on the end of the first pencil and try to lift the books. Move the fulcrum closer to, and then farther away from, the stack of books and try again. Display diagrams that show

the fulcrum in different positions, and describe how easily the books were lifted each time.

2. Observe and make a list of some common and important uses of first-class levers in daily life. Here are some examples:

- Playing on a see-saw

- Using a hammer to pull out a nail

- Using a tree branch to lift a rock

- Using a screwdriver to pry the lid off a paint can

Photographs and diagrams of these and other examples of first-class levers make a good project display.

CHECK IT OUT!

Find out about Archimedes, an ancient Greek scientist and mathematician, who first defined the principle of levers. What did he mean when he said "Give me a place to stand and I will move the earth"? Discover how he pulled a heavily loaded ship along the beach single-handedly.

Uphill

PROBLEM

How does an inclined plane (a flat, sloping surface) make lifting an object easier?

Materials

scissors
large rubber band
ruler
masking tape
3 books
yardstick (meterstick)
1 cup of rice
sock
string

Procedure

1. Make a scale as follows:

   • Cut the rubber band to form one long rubber strip.

   • Lay the rubber strip on a ruler. Pull the end of the strip over the edge of the ruler and tape it to the back of the ruler. Leave about 3 inches (7.6 cm) of the strip hanging down the front of the ruler.

2. Stack the books on a table.

3. Place one end of the yardstick (meterstick) on the edge of the books to form a ramp.

4. Pour the rice into the sock, and tie a knot in the sock.

5. Measure and cut a 12-inch (30-cm) piece of string.

6. Tie one end of the string to the free end of the rubber strip and the other end of the string around the top of the sock.

7. Place the sock on the surface of the table, and lift the scale straight up until the sock is at a height equal to that of the stacked books.

8. Observe the distance the rubber band stretches along the ruler.

9. Place the sock on the bottom part of the ramp.

10. Hold on to the scale, and slowly pull the sock to the top of the ramp.

11. Again, observe the distance the rubber band on the scale stretches as the sock is being pulled up the ramp.

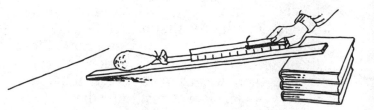

Results

The rubber band stretches a shorter distance when used to pull the sock full of rice up the ramp than when lifting the sock straight up.

Why?

The ramp is an **inclined plane** (a simple machine with a flat, sloping surface). It is used to move a load to a higher level with minimal effort. The length of the rubber band indicated that it took less effort force (the force you apply) to move the sock full of rice up the ramp than to lift it straight up. When using an inclined plane, you must move the load a greater distance than if you lifted it straight up, but it takes less effort force.

LET'S EXPLORE

1. Does the slant of the ramp affect the amount of effort required to move the sock to the top? Repeat the experiment twice, first increasing the slant by adding more books to the stack, and then decreasing the slant by using fewer books.

2. Does the surface of the ramp affect the results? Repeat the original experiment twice more, first taping wax paper across the yardstick (meterstick) to provide an extrasmooth surface, and then taping sandpaper across the stick to provide a rough surface. **Science Fair Hint:** Display the materials used and a summary of the results. In your written report about these results, include information about the difference in friction (the resistance to motion) between the rough and smooth surfaces.

SHOW TIME!

1. Use a hand-held scale to measure the amount of force required to lift a book straight up. Form an inclined plane by placing a board on the edge of the seat of a chair. Place the book on the bottom end of the ramp, and use the scale to pull the book up the ramp. Measure the effort force needed to pull the book up the ramp. Display photographs showing the book being held by the scale, and also being pulled up the ramp by the scale. Indicate the force required to lift the book straight up and to pull it up the ramp.

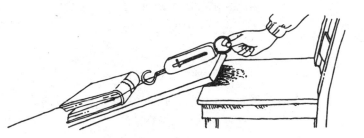

2. Take a closer look at the world around you. Observe and discover common inclined planes—such as stairs, wheelchair ramps, roads winding up and around a mountain, and ramps at loading docks—used to move objects to higher levels. Photographs of different kinds of inclined planes, along with pictures from magazines, can be used as part of a project display.

CHECK IT OUT!

More than 2,000 years ago the Egyptians built tombs for the pharaohs. Some of the tombs are more than 400 feet (120 m) tall. The largest, built by the pharaoh Khufu, has at least 2,300,000 carefully cut and exactly laid stones weighing about 3,000 pounds (1,362 kg) each. Read about the pyramids and find out how the Egyptians used inclined planes to place these large stone blocks one on top of the other.

Attractive

PROBLEM

What materials are attracted to a magnet?

Materials

testing materials: aluminum foil, copper wire, glass marble, steel nail, paper, steel BBs, wooden match
bar magnet

Procedure

1. Lay the testing materials on a *wooden* table.

2. Touch the magnet to, and slowly move the magnet away from, each material.

3. Observe and record which materials cling to the magnet.

Results

The nail and the BBs are the only materials that cling to the magnet.

Why?

A **magnet** is a substance that is made of and can attract magnetic materials. **Magnetic materials** are attracted by a magnet and include iron, cobalt, nickel, and mixtures of these metals with each other and/or other substances.

The attraction that magnets have for magnetic materials, and the attraction and repulsion between magnetic poles are called **magnetic force.** Magnetic force is also called magnetism. The area around a magnet where the magnetic force acts is called the **magnetic field.** The atoms in magnetic substances cluster together in groups called magnetic domains. A **magnetic domain** is a region in which the atoms are arranged so that their magnetic fields line up to form a larger magnetic field. The domains inside magnetic materials act like tiny magnets with a **north** and a **south pole** (opposite ends of a magnet).

LET'S EXPLORE

1. Are BBs and steel nails the only magnetic materials? Repeat the experiment using testing materials that are not on the materials list. Keep a record of the materials that are found to be magnetic. **Science Fair Hint:** This record can be used as part of a written report to be displayed with your project.

2. Does the magnet have to touch the testing material to attract it? Repeat the original experiment, holding the magnet very near, but not touching, the materials. **Science Fair Hint:** Display photographs taken during the experiment that show magnets

held at different distances from each testing material. Include photos of magnetic materials clinging to a magnet, and record a measurement of the height the material moved to reach the magnet. Try to determine which materials have the strongest magnetic properties.

SHOW TIME!

1. Using a steel nail and a paper clip that has not been near a magnet, test the attraction of the nail for the paper clip. Then, **magnetize** (to make magnetic) the nail by laying it on a magnet for 1 or more minutes. Test the attraction of the paper clip to the magnetized nail. Prepare a poster showing the domains of the magnetized and unmagnetized nail. Indicate on your poster the attraction of a paper clip to the different nails.

2. As part of an oral presentation, demonstrate how a magnet can be used to separate magnetic and nonmagnetic materials. Combine 1 teaspoon (5 ml) of salt and 1 teaspoon (5 ml) of iron filings. (You can find iron filings inside some magnetic

drawing toys sold at toy stores.) Pour the mixture onto a sheet of paper. Pass a bar magnet near, but not touching, the surface of the mixture. The iron filings will cling to the magnet and the salt will stay on the paper.

CHECK IT OUT!

The ability of magnets to separate magnetic materials from nonmagnetic materials is important in many industries. Read about magnets and prepare a chart showing what you have learned. Here are some examples of magnets being used as separators:

- Metals separated from ore

- Archaeologists recovering sunken treasure from the ocean floor with a magnetic sweeper

- Food manufacturers preventing small iron particles that rub off of machinery from mixing with food

- Vendors sorting nonmagnetic coins from magnetic slugs and washers that are dropped into vending machines

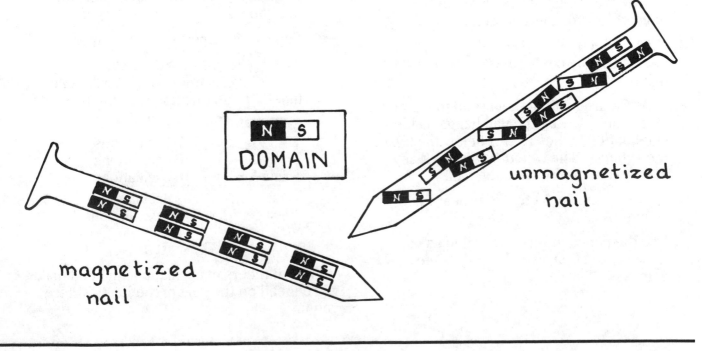

DOMAIN

magnetized nail

unmagnetized nail

Back and Forth

PROBLEM

How can you measure the Earth's magnetism at different locations?

Materials

sheet of paper
masking tape
small iron nail
bar magnet
scissors
ruler
thread
compass
pencil
timer

Procedure

1. Roll the paper and tape it to form a large open-ended cylinder. Place the cylinder on the floor next to a *wooden* table.

2. Magnetize the nail by laying it on the magnet for 1 or more minutes.

3. Cut a 36-inch (1-m) piece of thread, and tie one end to the center of the magnetized nail.

4. Tape the free end of the thread to the edge of the table so that the nail hangs inside and about 2 inches (5 cm) below the top of the cylinder. The cylinder will block any breeze that might move the nail.

5. Set the compass on the floor near the cylinder.

6. Use the pencil to turn the nail in an east-to-west direction, as indicated by the compass.

7. Ask a helper to start the timer when the nail is released. Have your helper announce the end of 1 minute.

8. Count the number of **oscillations** (one back-and-forth movement of a free-swinging object) the nail makes during 1 minute.

9. Repeat the experiment twice more.

10. Average the results of the three trials by adding the number of oscillations together and dividing the sum by three.

Example:

Trial #1	17 oscillations
Trial #2	16 oscillations
Trial #3	18 oscillations
Total	51 oscillations

Average: 51 ÷ 3 = 17 oscillations

Results

The numbers of oscillations the nail makes will depend on the part of the Earth where you live.

Why?

Earth behaves like a huge magnet, and its ends are the magnetic north and magnetic south poles. The **magnetic north** and **magnetic south poles** of Earth attract the poles (ends) of a free-swinging magnet, such as a compass needle. The north pole of the compass needle points to the magnetic north pole and the south pole to the magnetic south pole. The number of oscillations made by a hanging magnet, such as the magnetized nail, varies with the distance you are from either pole. The closer you are to any one magnetic pole, the greater will be the oscillation of the magnet.

LET'S EXPLORE

1. Would a different-size nail affect the number of oscillations? Repeat the experiment twice, first using a smaller nail, and then using a larger nail.

2. Does the size of the thread affect the oscillation of the nail? Repeat the original experiment using a thicker string to suspend the nail.

3. Is there a difference in the strength of the Earth's magnetic field in your neighborhood? Repeat the original experiment at different locations, such as at school or at the homes of friends. If you have the opportunity to travel, take the materials with you and measure the Earth's magnetism in a different town. **Science Fair Hint:** Make a map of the area where you performed the experiment, with the results of the experiment printed on it. A summary stating the results should be printed at the bottom of the map.

SHOW TIME!

Simulate the testing of the Earth's magnetic field closer to its magnetic poles by placing a magnet near the hanging nail. Count the oscillations of the nail with the magnet at different distances from the nail. Use this experiment as part of your display. Attach the string to a support placed across the top of your project display, with the nail hanging freely in the center of the project. Use a magnet to demonstrate the change in the speed of the oscillations as the strength of the magnetic field increases.

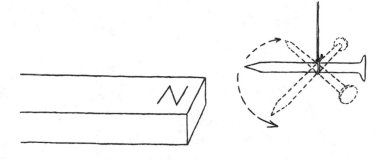

CHECK IT OUT!

Conduct special research of the measurement of the Earth's magnetic field. With the assistance of your parents and teacher, you can correspond with students in different geographic locations. In previous experiments, you determined if the size of the nail and string affected the results. Use the results of these experiments to instruct your "around-the-world laboratory helpers" about the type of materials needed for their testings. The results can be displayed as a science fair project.

Mathematics

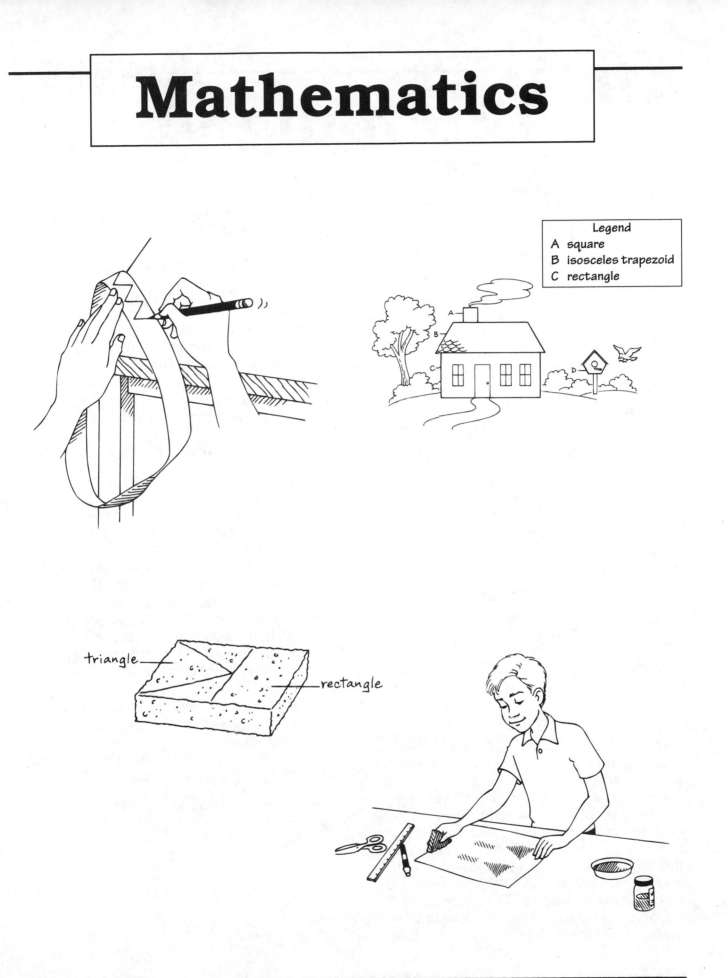

Legend
A square
B isosceles trapezoid
C rectangle

triangle

rectangle

Unchanged

PROBLEM

What is topology?

Materials

walnut-size piece of modeling clay

Procedure

1. Shape the clay into a ball.

2. Tap the clay ball against a hard surface, such as a table, to shape it into a cube.

3. Mold the cube into the shape of a gingerbread man without breaking the clay.

4. Make a diagram of the changes in the clay similar to the one shown here.

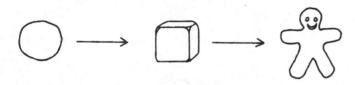

Results

Different figures are made by molding the clay.

Why?

Topology is a branch of geometry that studies properties of geometric figures that remain unchanged when the shape of the figures is gradually changed. Figures are said to be **topologically equivalent** if they can be obtained from one another without cutting the figure or punching a hole. In this experiment, the ball is molded into a cube that is molded into a gingerbread man. All three figures are topologically equivalent. The property that remains unchanged about all three figures is that each has zero holes. In topology, the number of holes in a figure is called its **genus.** The figures in this experiment all have a genus of zero.

LET'S EXPLORE

A figure with a genus of one indicates that it has one hole through it. Repeat the experiment, starting with a clay figure in the shape of a donut. Form topologically equivalent figures, such as a needle (hole is the eye), cup (hole is the handle), or funnel (hole through the center). **Science Fair Hint:** Prepare a poster showing figures with different genus.

SHOW TIME!

1a. Another example of what topology studies is the Möbius strip. This loop, named after its discoverer, the German mathematician August Ferdinand Möbius (1790–1868), appears to have two sides, but actually has only one. This property does not change if the strip's shape is changed (within the restrictions that it is not cut or its genus changed). To make a Möbius strip, take a 36-inch (1-m) strip of adding machine tape, give one end half a turn, and tape the ends together. Prove that the strip has only one side by laying the strip over the corner of a table. Starting where the edges are taped together, draw a zigzag line back and forth down the strip until you return to the starting point.

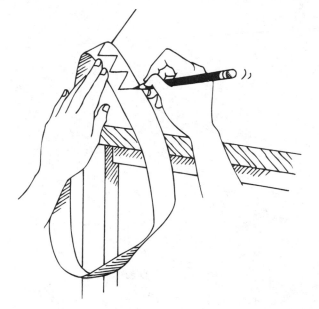

b. The Möbius strip has only one side and one edge. Mark the strip again, this time using a colored pen to mark along one edge of the paper.

c. The Möbius strip has one half-twist, which is an odd number. If the number of half-twists is odd, will a loop with

more than one half-twist have more than one surface and one edge, as does the Möbius strip? Repeat steps 1a and 1b twice, first using a loop with 3 half-twists, then using a loop with 5 half-twists.

d. How would an even number of half-twists in a loop affect its number of surfaces and edges? Repeat steps 1a and 1b two or more times, using a loop with 2, 4, 6, or any even number of half-twists.

e. Let T represent the number of half-twists in a loop. Make and display a poster with drawings for loops where T = 0, T = 1, T = 2. Indicate the number of surfaces and edges for each drawing.

CHECK IT OUT!

One of the branches of topology deals with the drawing of figures with one continuous stroke of a pencil—that is, without lifting the pencil or tracing a line twice. How can one determine if a figure can be traced in this manner? For information, see pages 95–102 in *Janice VanCleave's Geometry for Every Kid* (New York: Wiley, 1994).

Polys

PROBLEM

What is a polygon?

Materials

marking pen
ruler
rectangular dishwashing sponge
scissors
poster paint (any color)
small bowl
sheet of white construction paper

Procedure

1. Use the pen and ruler to draw a line across the center of the sponge, dividing the sponge into two equal sections.

2. Draw a triangle on one section of the sponge.

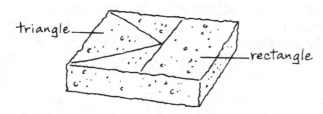

3. Cut out the two indicated shapes drawn on the sponge. Keep the triangle for this experiment and the rectangular piece for the following "Let's Explore" experiment. Discard the remaining sponge pieces.

4. Pour about ½ inch (1.25 cm) of paint into the bowl.

5. Look at the sides of the triangle. Dip one of the large triangular faces into the bowl of paint, and make a print of this face on the paper.

6. Turn the sponge over and make a print of the opposite face.

7. Repeat steps 5 and 6 to make prints of the remaining sides of the sponge.

Results

Five prints with two different kinds of shapes are made.

Why?

A **polygon** is a **closed figure** (a geometric figure that begins and ends at the same point) formed by three or more straight line segments that are joined only where the ends of the line segments meet. Each of these endpoints is connected to only two line segments. A polygon made of three sides is called a **triangle.** The sum of the angles created by the three sides of a triangle is always 180 degrees. A polygon made of four sides with two pairs of parallel sides and **right angles** (angles that measure 90 degrees) is called a **rectangle.** Two of the prints made with the sponge are triangles and three are rectangles.

LET'S EXPLORE

A **quadrilateral** is a four-sided polygon formed by four line segments. One type of quadrilateral is a **parallelogram,** which has two pairs of parallel sides. A rectangle is an example of a parallelogram. How many different-size parallelogram prints can be made by the rectangular sponge from the experiment? Repeat the experiment, using the rectangular sponge and a different color of paint. **Science**

Fair Hint: Use the prints to prepare a display representing polygons.

SHOW TIME!

1. There are three basic types of quadrilaterals: the **trapezium,** which has no parallel sides; the **trapezoid,** which has one pair of parallel sides; and the parallelogram. Prepare and display a chart representing the different types of quadrilaterals and examples of each, such as the one shown here. Prepare a legend giving a description of each example. For information, see pages 37–42 in *Janice VanCleave's Geometry for Every Kid.* (New York: Wiley, 1994).

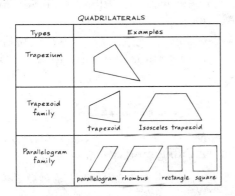

2. A **rhomboid** is a parallelogram that has no right angles and only opposite sides are **congruent** (the same). A rhomboid is like a flexible rectangle with its top pushed to one side and its bottom to the other. The shape of a rhomboid can be changed into that of an equal-size rectangle by cutting off a triangle from one side and placing it on the opposite side. Demonstrate this by drawing a large rhomboid on a sheet of paper. Use a ruler to draw a perpendicular dashed line from the top left **vertex** (point where two lines meet) of the rhomboid to its base. This line forms a triangle shape. Draw stripes across the triangle then cut along the dashed line and move the cutaway triangle to the opposite side of the rhomboid.

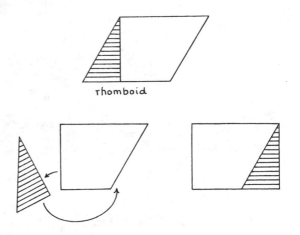

3. Polyhedrons are three-dimensional figures with flat surfaces called **faces.** These faces are polygons. Display drawings of polyhedrons, such as a house or a cereal box. Label the different polygons on the drawings.

CHECK IT OUT!

A *tanagram* is a Chinese puzzle made by cutting a square into seven polygons: five triangles, one square, one rhomboid. The pieces can be arranged to form the original square as well as a great variety of other polygons. For information about making and creating different polygons with a tanagram, see pages 101–104 in Margaret Kenda and Phyllis S. Williams's *Math Wizardry for Kids* (Hauppauge, NY: Barron's, 1995).

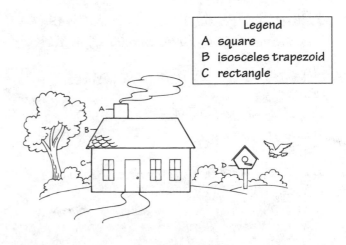

Science Project and Experiment Books

ASTRONOMY

VanCleave, Janice. *Astronomy for Every Kid*. New York: Wiley, 1991.

Wood, Robert W. *Science for Kids: 39 Easy Astronomy Experiments*. Blue Ridge Summit, PA: TAB Books, 1991.

BIOLOGY

Bonnet, Robert L., and G. Daniel Keen. *Botany: 49 Science Fair Projects*. Blue Ridge Summit, PA: TAB Books, 1989.

———. *Botany: 49 More Science Fair Projects*. Blue Ridge Summit, PA: TAB Books, 1989.

Cain, Nancy Woodard. *Animal Behavior Science Projects*. New York: Wiley, 1995.

Dashefsky, H. Steven. *Zoology: 49 Science Fair Projects*. Blue Ridge Summit, PA: TAB Books, 1995.

Hershey, David R. *Plant Biology Science Projects*. New York: Wiley, 1995.

Kneidel, Sally. *Pet Bugs*. New York: Wiley, 1994.

Russo, Monica. *The Insect Almanac*. New York: Sterling, 1992.

VanCleave, Janice. *A+ Biology*. New York: Wiley, 1993.

———. *Animals*. New York: Wiley, 1993.

———. *Biology for Every Kid*. New York: Wiley, 1990.

———. *The Human Body for Every Kid*. New York: Wiley, 1995.

———. *Foods and Nutrition for Every Kid*. New York: Wiley, 1999.

———. *Insects*. New York: Wiley, 1998.

———. *Microscopes and Magnifying Lenses*. New York: Wiley, 1993.

———. *Plants*. New York: Wiley, 1997.

Wood, Robert W. *Science for Kids: 39 Easy Animal Biology Experiments*. Blue Ridge Summit, PA: TAB Books, 1991.

———. *Science for Kids: 39 Easy Plant Biology Experiments*. Blue Ridge Summit, PA: TAB Books, 1991.

CHEMISTRY

Johnson, Mary. *Chemistry Experiments*. London: Usborn Publishing, 1981.

VanCleave, Janice. *Chemistry for Every Kid*. New York: Wiley, 1989.

———. *A+ Chemistry*. New York: Wiley, 1993.

———. *Molecules*. New York: Wiley, 1993.

EARTH SCIENCE

Levine, Shar, and Allison Grafton. *Projects for a Healthy Planet*. New York: Wiley, 1992.

VanCleave, Janice. *A+ Earth Science*. New York: Wiley, 1999.

———. *Dinosaurs for Every Kid*. New York: Wiley, 1994.

———. *Earthquakes. New York:* Wiley, 1993.

———. *Earth Science for Every Kid*. New York: Wiley, 1991.

———. *Ecology for Every Kid*. New York: Wiley, 1995.

———. *Geography for Every Kid.* New York: Wiley, 1993.

———. *Oceanography for Every Kid.* New York: Wiley, 1995.

———. *Rocks and Minerals.* New York: Wiley, 1996.

———. *Solar Systems. New York:* Wiley, 2000.

———. *Volcanoes. New York:* Wiley, 1994.

———. *Weather. New York:* Wiley, 1995.

Wood, Robert W. *Science for Kids: 39 Easy Geology Experiments.* Blue Ridge Summit, PA: TAB Books, 1991.

———. *Science for Kids: 39 Easy Meteorology Experiments.* Blue Ridge Summit, PA: TAB Books, 1991.

MATH

VanCleave, Janice. *Geometry for Every Kid.* New York: Wiley, 1994.

———. *Math for Every Kid.* New York: Wiley, 1991.

PHYSICS

Amery, Heather, and Angela Littler. *The How Book of Batteries and Magnets.* London: Usborn Publishing, 1989.

Cobb, Vicki. *Science Experiments You Can Eat.* New York: HarperTrophy, 1994.

VanCleave, Janice. *Electricity.* New York: Wiley, 1994.

———. *Gravity.* New York: Wiley, 1993.

———. *Machines.* New York: Wiley, 1993.

———. *Magnets.* New York: Wiley, 1993.

———. *Physics for Every Kid.* New York: Wiley, 1991.

Wiese, Jim. *Roller Coaster Science.* New York: Wiley, 1994.

Wood, Robert W. *Sound Fundamentals.* New York: Learning Triangle Press, 1997.

GENERAL PROJECT AND EXPERIMENT BOOKS

Amato, Carol J. *Super Science Fair Projects.* Chicago: Contemporary Books, 1994.

Bochinski, Julianne Blair. *The Complete Book of Science Fair Projects,* revised edition. New York: Wiley, 1996.

Bombaugh, Ruth. *Science Fair Success.* Hillside, NJ: Enslow, 1990.

Cobb, Vicki. *Science Experiments You Can Eat.* New York: HarperTrophy, 1994.

Frekko, Janet, and Phyllis Katz. *Great Science Fair Projects.* New York: Watts, 1992.

Levine, Shar, and Leslie Johnstone. *Everyday Science.* New York: Wiley, 1995.

———. *Silly Science.* New York: Wiley, 1995.

Markle, Sandra. *The Young Scientist's Guide to Successful Science Projects.* New York: Beech Tree Books, 1990.

Murphy, Pat, Ellen Klages, Linda Shore, and the Staff of the Exploratorium. *The Science Explorer.* New York: Henry Holt and Co., 1996.

Potter, Jean. *Science in Seconds for Kids.* New York: Wiley, 1995.

Smolinski, Jill. 50 *Nifty Super Science Fair Projects.* Los Angeles: Lowell House Juvenile, 1995.

VanCleave, Janice. *Guide to the Best Science Fair Projects.* New York: Wiley, 1997.

———. *200 Gooey, Slippery, Slimy, Weird, and Fun Experiments.* New York: Wiley, 1993.

———. *201 Awesome, Magical, Bizarre, and Incredible Experiments.* New York: Wiley, 1994.

———. *202 Oozing, Bubbling, Dripping, and Bouncing Experiments.* New York: Wiley, 1996.

Vacchione, Glen. *100 Amazing Make-It-Yourself Science Fair Projects.* New York: Sterling, 1994.

Wood, Robert W. *When? Experiments for the Young Scientist.* Blue Ridge Summit, PA: TAB Books, 1995.

Reference Books

ASTRONOMY

Beasane, Pam. *1000 Facts about Space.* New York: Kingfisher, 1992.

Harrington, Philip, and Edward Pascuzzi. *Astronomy for All Ages.* Old Saybrook, CT: Globe Pequot Press, 1994.

Moche, Dinah L. *Astronomy: A Self-Teaching Guide.* New York: Wiley, 1989.

Pearce, Q. L. *Stargazer's Guide to the Galaxy.* New York: Doherty, 1991.

BIOLOGY

Garber, Steven D. *Biology: A Self-Teaching Guide.* New York: Wiley, 1989.

Stein, Sara. *The Body Book.* New York: Workman, 1992.

CHEMISTRY

Tocci, Salvatore. *Chemistry Around You.* New York: Prentice Hall, 1985.

EARTH SCIENCE

Dennis, Jerry. *It's Raining Frogs and Fishes.* New York: Harper Perennial, 1992.

Forrester, Frank H. *1001 Questions Answered about the Weather.* New York: Dover, 1981.

Groves, Don. *The Oceans.* New York: Wiley, 1989.

Lockhart, Gary. *The Weather Companion.* New York: Wiley, 1988.

Tufty, Barbara. *1001 Questions Answered about Hurricanes, Tornadoes, and Other Natural Air Disasters.* New York: Dover, 1989.

ENGINEERING

Editors of Consumer Guide. *The Big Book of How Things Work.* Lincoln Wood, IL: Publications International, 1991.

Parker, Steve. *How Things Work.* New York: Random House, 1991.

Schwartz, Max. *Machines, Buildings, Weaponry of Biblical Times.* Old Tappan, NJ: Revell, 1990.

Williams, Brian. *Science and Technology.* New York: Kingfisher, 1993.

GENERAL SCIENCE

Bosak, Susan V. *Science Is.* New York: Scholastic, 1991.

Feldman, David. *How Does Aspirin Find a Headache?* New York: Harper Perennial, 1994.

Holzinger, Philip R. *The House of Science.* New York: Wiley, 1990.

Kerrod, Robin. *Book of Science.* New York: Simon and Schuster, 1991.

Roberts, Royston M., and Jeanie Roberts. *Lucky Science.* New York: Wiley, 1995.

MATH

Kenda, Margaret, and Phyllis S. Williams. *Math Wizardry for Kids.* Hauppauge, NY: Barron's, 1995.

Salem, Lionel, Frederic Testard, and Coralie Salem. *The Most Beautiful Mathematical Formulas.* New York: Wiley, 1992.

PHYSICS

Bohren, Craig F. *What Light through Yonder Window Breaks?* New York: Wiley, 1991.

Walker, Jearl. *The Flying Circus of Physics with Answers.* New York: Wiley, 1977.

Sources of Scientific Supplies

CATALOG SUPPLIERS

Carolina Biological Supply Company
2700 York Road
Burlington, NC 27215
(800) 334-5551

Cuisenaire
10 Bank Street
P.O. Box 5026
White Plains, NY 10606
(800) 237-3142

Delta Education, Inc.
P.O. Box 915
Hudson, NH 03051-0915
(800) 258-1302

Fisher Scientific
Educational Materials Division
485 South Frontage Road
Burr Ridge, IL 60521
(708) 655-4410
(800) 766-7000

Frey Scientific Division of Beckley Cardy
100 Paragon Parkway
Mansfield, OH 44903
(800) 225-3739

NASCO
901 Janesville Avenue
P.O. Box 901
Fort Atkinson, WI 53538
(800) 677-2960

Sargent-Welch
911 Commerce Court
Buffalo Grove, IL 60089
(800) 727-4368

Showboard
P.O. Box 10656
Tampa, FL 33679-0656
(800) 323-9189

Ward's Natural Science
5100 West Henrietta Road
Rochester, NY 14586
(800) 962-2660

SOURCES OF ROCKS AND MINERALS

The following stores carry rocks and minerals and are located in many areas. To find the stores near you, call the home offices listed below.

Mineral of the Month Club
1290 Ellis Avenue
Cambria, CA 93428
(800) 941-5594
cambriaman@thegrid.net
www.mineralofthemonthclub.com

Nature Company
750 Hearst Avenue
Berkeley, CA 94701
(800) 227-1114

Nature of Things
10700 West Venture Drive
Franklin, WI 53132–2804
(800) 283-2921

The Discovery Store
15046 Beltway Drive
Dallas, TX 75244
(214) 490-8299

World of Science
900 Jefferson Road
Building 4
Rochester, NY 14623
(716) 475-0100

Glossary

abdomen The rear part of an insect's body.

abrasion Weathering process in which rocks rub against each other, wear each other down, or break into smaller pieces.

absorb To take in.

acid A substance that yields positive hydrogen particles when dissolved in water.

acid rain Rain with a higher than normal amount of acid; caused when rain reacts with acid gases from automobile exhausts and factories.

albedo The reflecting ability of a celestial body.

altitude The angular height above the horizon.

amylase A chemical found in saliva that breaks down starch into less complex chemicals.

analyze To examine carefully and in detail.

anatomy The study of animals and animal life.

anemometer An instrument used to measure how fast the wind blows.

angiosperm Flowering plants that have a covered seed.

annular eclipse When the Moon is far enough from Earth to appear smaller than the Sun, resulting in a rim of light seen around the eclipsed Sun.

antenna (pl. **antennae**) Moveable part of an insect's head used to smell, feel, and sometimes to hear with.

apparent brightness How bright a celestial body appears to be as observed from the Earth.

astronomy The study of the solar system, stars, and the universe.

atmosphere The layer of gas surrounding a celestial body.

atom The building block of matter; the smallest part of an element retaining the element's properties.

auxin A plant chemical that causes plant cells to elongate.

bar graph A diagram that uses bars to represent data.

base Substance that yields a negative hydroxyl ion when dissolved in water.

beach A shore with a smooth, sloping stretch of sand and pebbles.

behaviorism The study of actions that alter the relationship between an organism, such as a plant or an animal, and its environment.

binocular vision The ability to combine images viewed by two eyes; produces three-dimensional vision.

biology The study of plants and plant life, including their structure and growth.

bond A connection between atoms.

botany The study of plants and plant life, including their structure and growth.

calibrate To determine and mark the position of individual measuring marks on an instrument such as a thermometer.

camouflage Colors and/or patterns that conceal an object by matching its background.

carbon dioxide Part of the gases making up air; produced by burning fuels and exhaled by animals.

celestial bodies Natural objects in the sky such as stars, suns, moons, and planets.

cell The basic building block of all living things.

cell membrane The thin, filmlike outer layer of a cell that holds the cell together and separates it from its environment.

cell wall The stiff outer layer of a plant cell.

cerebellum The part of the brain that coordinates all the muscle actions.

cerebrum The largest and most complex part of the brain; where all thought occurs and where input messages from nerves are interpreted.

chart Data or other information in the form of a table, graph, or list.

chemical compound A combination of two or more different elements.

chemical weathering The breaking down of rock by a change in its chemical composition.

chemistry The study of the materials that substances are made of and how they change and combine.

chlorophyll Green pigment located in the chloroplasts of plants; necessary for photosynthesis.

chloroplast A green body in plant cells that gives plants their green color and in which food for the plant is made.

cleavage The tendency of a mineral to break along a smooth surface.

cleavage plane The area of a mineral where it can be easily split apart

climate Average weather in a region over a long period of time.

closed figure A geometric figure that begins and ends at the same point.

compression forces Forces pushing toward each other from opposite directions.

condensation The process of a gas changing to a liquid.

condenses Changes from a gas to a liquid.

congruent The same; equal to.

contract Get smaller; to squeeze together.

control A test in which the independent variable is kept constant in order to measure changes in the dependent variable.

controlled variable Something that is kept the same in an experiment.

core The innermost, hottest layer of the Earth.

core sample A usually cylinder-shaped section cut from the Earth's crust that reveals the materials at different depths.

cotyledon A simple leaf that stores food for a developing plant; also called a seed leaf.

coxa The leg segment connected to an insect's body.

crescent phase Phase of the Moon with small lighted area resembling a segment of a ring with pointed ends.

crust The relatively thin, outermost, coolest part of the Earth.

crystal A solid made up of atoms arranged in an orderly, regular pattern; a recognizable shape that results from the repetition of the same combination of atomic particles.

culms Upright grass stems aboveground.

current A swift stream of water or air.

cytoplasm The jellylike material, made mostly of water, that fills a cell.

darkling beetle An often dark-colored beetle that eats vegetable matter. The larval stage is known as a mealworm.

data In this book, data is observations and/or measured facts obtained experimentally.

dehydrate To lose water.

density A measurement of how much mass is packed into a certain volume.

dependent variable The variable being observed in an experiment that changes in response to the independent variable.

dicot or **dicotyledon** An angiosperm whose seeds have two cotyledons.

digest To break down food into useable forms.

displacement Movement from one place to another.

earth science The study of the Earth.

earthshine Sunlight reflected off the Earth.

earthquake Violent shaking of the Earth caused by a sudden movement of rock beneath its surface.

eclipse When one object passes in front of and blocks the light of another object.

ecology The study of the relationships of living things to other living things and to their environment.

effort arm The distance from the fulcrum to the point on a lever where you apply force.

effort force The push or pull needed to move an object.

electrically neutral Containing an equal number of positive and negative charges.

electricity The form of energy associated with the presence and/or the movement of electric charges.

electromagnetic radiation Energy in the form of waves that can travel through space, including radio waves and light waves.

electron A negative charge.

element Matter that is made of only one kind of atom.

embryo Partially developed plant inside a seed.

engineering The application of scientific knowledge for practical purposes.

epicotyl Part of a plant embryo that develops into stems, leaves, flowers, and fruit.

erosion The process that includes weathering and the displacement of weathered material by natural forces, such as wind, rain, water, and ice.

exhale Breathing out.

exoskeleton The outer body covering of an insect; external skeleton.

expand To get larger.

exploratory experiments As defined in this book, experiments in which the data is part of the research.

faces Flat surfaces of a three-dimensional object.

femur The second main segment of an insect's leg.

first-class lever A bar with the fulcrum between the load and the effort. The effort force is increased by this simple machine when the effort arm is longer that the load arm.

flexible The ability of a material to bend or stretch without breaking.

flower Plant organ for producing more plants.

foraminifera Tiny ocean creatures with shells that differ in shape and makeup depending on the climate in which they were formed; they give scientists clues to major climate changes over time.

fossilized Hardened trace of an organism from past geologic times.

fossils Traces of the remains of prehistoric animals and plants.

fracture A way in which a mineral breaks other than along a smooth surface; uneven breaking.

friction The resistance to motion between two surfaces that are touching each other.

frost action The weathering of rock as a result of repeated freezing and thawing of water.

fulcrum The fixed point of rotation on a lever.

fungal Referring to plantlike organisms called fungi, which cannot make their own food.

gas The phase of matter with no definite volume or shape.

genus   The number of holes in a geometric figure.

geology   The study of the composition of the Earth's layers and its history. See also the subtopics **mineralogy, seismology, volcanology, fossils,** and **rocks.**

geometry   The branch of mathematics that deals with points, lines, planes, and their relationships to one another.

geotropism   The growth response of plants to gravity.

germination   The process by which a seed embryo develops.

germination starting time (GST)   As defined in this book, the time it takes from planting a seed to the first signs of hypocotyl growth.

germination time (GT)   As defined in this book, the time it takes from planting a seed to the end of germination, determined by the time it takes for the epicotyl to fully emerge from the cotyledons.

gravity   The force of attraction between two bodies; the force that pulls objects toward the center of Earth.

greenhouse   Structure designed to provide a protected, controlled environment for raising plants indoors.

greenhouse effect   Warming of a planet due to absorption and release of infrared waves by molecules in the atmosphere.

half-life   The time it takes for half of the mass of a radioactive element to decay.

head   For insects, the front section.

hurricane   A tropical storm with winds of 74 miles (118 km) per hour or more that rotate around a relatively calm center.

hydrocarbon   Molecule containing hydrogen and carbon atoms.

hypocotyl   The part of a plant embryo that develops into roots.

hypothesis   An idea about the solution to a problem, based on knowledge and research.

iceberg   A large mass of floating ice in the ocean.

immiscible liquids   Liquids that are not able to mix together.

inclined plane   A simple machine with a flat, sloping surface.

independent variable   A manipulated variable in an experiment that causes a change in the dependent variable.

indicator   A chemical that changes color in acid and/or base.

inertia   Resistance to change in motion.

infrared radiation   Heat waves; long-wavelength electromagnetic radiation.

inhale   Breathing in.

inorganic   Describes substances not formed from the remains of living organisms.

insect   Small animals with three pairs of jointed legs and three body parts: head, thorax, and abdomen.

internode   The area on a plant stem between two consecutive nodes.

joint   Where different parts fit together.

journal   A written record of your project from start to finish.

kinetic energy   Energy of motion.

lateral   Side-to-side.

lateral brace   Horizontal support between two vertical structures.

leaf   A special plant organ for manufacturing food.

lever   A rigid bar used to lift or move things. It has three basic parts: a load, an effort force, and a fulcrum. It is a machine that does work by pivoting around a fixed point called a fulcrum.

line graph   A diagram that uses lines to express patterns of change.

liquid   The phase of matter with a definite volume but no definite shape.

lithosphere   The solid part of the Earth, made up of the crust and the upper part of the mantle.

load   The object moved by a machine.

load arm   The distance on a lever from the fulcrum to the load being supported.

luminous   Gives off light.

lungs   Breathing organs.

machine   Device that makes work easier; device that changes either the direction or the amount of force that you must apply to accomplish a task.

magma   Liquid rock beneath the surface of the Earth.

magnet   A substance that can attract iron or other magnetic material; magnetic material in which its domains line up in the same direction.

magnetic domain   A region in which atoms are arranged so that their magnetic fields line up to form a larger magnetic field.

magnetic field   The area around a magnet where the magnetic force acts.

magnetic force   The attraction that magnets have for magnetic materials, and the attraction and repulsion between magnetic poles; also called magnetism.

magnetic material   Materials that are attracted to magnets, including iron, cobalt, nickel, and mixtures of these metals with each other and/or other substances.

magnetic poles   The magnetic poles are points on the Earth that attract a compass needle; magnetic north pole and magnetic south pole.

magnetism   See **magnetic force.**

magnetize   To make magnetic.

magnitude   Measurement of the amount of shaking energy released by an earthquake.

mantle   The second layer of the Earth; hotter than the crust but cooler than the core.

mass   An amount of material.

mathematics   The use of numbers and symbols to study amounts and forms. See also **geometry**.

matter   Anything that has mass.

mealworm   A growing stage of a darkling beetle.

membranous   Resembling a thin, flexible sheet of tissue paper.

meteorologist   Scientist who studies weather.

meteorology   The study of weather, climate, and the earth's atmosphere.

microbiology   The study of microscopic organisms, such as fungi, bacteria, and protista.

mineral   A single, solid element or chemical compound found in the Earth that makes up rock and that has four basic characteristics: (1) it occurs naturally; (2) it is inorganic; (3) it is has a definite chemical composition; and (4) it has a crystalline structure.

mineralogy   The study of the composition and formation of minerals.

mitochondria (sing. **mitochondrion)**   The power stations of a cell, where food and oxygen combine to produce the energy needed for the cell to work and live.

molecules   Smallest part of a substance that keeps the properties of that substance; contains two or more atoms.

molting   The process of shedding an exoskeleton.

monocot or monocotyledon   An angiosperm whose seeds have one cotyledon.

mouthparts   Body parts on the head of an insect used to gather and eat food.

nectar   Sugary liquid of flowers.

negative geotropism   Plant growth in a direction opposite the pull of gravity.

nerve   Special bundles of cells that the body uses to carry messages to and from the brain; messages are also carried to and from the spinal cord, a bundle of nerves running down the back.

neutral solution   One that is neither acidic nor basic.

node   A joint in a plant stem where a leaf is generally attached.

north pole   End of a free-swinging magnet, such as a compass needle that points to Earth's north magnetic pole.

nucleus   The control center of a cell that directs all the cell's activities; center of an atom.

nutrients   Materials needed for life and growth of living things.

oceanography   The study of the oceans and marine organisms.

orbit   The curved path of one body around another.

organ   Structure consisting of different tissues grouped to perform a specific function or functions.

organism   All living things, including people, plants, animals, and tiny living things called bacteria and fungi.

oscillation   One back-and-forth movement of a free-swinging object.

oxidation   The chemical process by which oxygen combines with other substances.

oxygen   A gas in the air.

ozone   A form of oxygen that contains three combined oxygen atoms.

ozone layer   Concentrated layer of ozone found between 10 and 20 miles (16 and 32 km) above the Earth's surface.

paleontology   The study of prehistoric life-forms.

parallelogram   A quadrilateral with two pairs of parallel sides.

partial solar eclipse   When an observer is in the penumbra of the Moon's shadow. Only part of the Sun is eclipsed.

penumbra   The lighter outer region of a shadow.

perimeter   The measurement of a boundary of an area.

peripheral vision   Vision to the side.

photometer   An instrument that measures the brightness of light.

photosphere   Bright visible surface of the Sun.

photosynthesis   The process by which plants use light and chlorophyll to change water and carbon dioxide into food.

physical science   The study of matter and energy.

physical weathering   The breakdown of rock without any changes in its chemical composition.

physics   The study of forms of energy and the laws of motion. See also **electricity, energy, gravity, machines,** and **magnetism.**

physiology   The study of life processes, such as respiration, circulation, the nervous system, metabolism, and reproduction.

pictograph   A chart that contains symbols representing data.

pie chart   A circle graph that shows information in percentages.

pigment   Substances that absorb, reflect, and transmit visible light.

pithy   Soft and spongy.

polygon   A closed figure formed by three or more line segments that are joined only where the ends of the line segments meet. Each of these endpoints is connected to only two line segments.

polyhedron A three-dimensional object with polygon faces.

positive geotropism Plant growth in the direction of the pull of gravity.

predator An animal that kills and eats other animals.

primary research Information collected on one's own.

problem A scientific question to be solved.

proboscis The tubelike mouthpart of some insects.

project conclusion A summary of the results of the project experimentation and a statement of how the results relate to the hypothesis.

project experiment An experiment designed to test a hypothesis.

project report The written record of your entire project from start to finish.

project research Research to help you understand the project topic, express a problem, propose a hypothesis, and design one or more project experiments.

propagate To produce new organisms.

protective coloration Coloring that helps to protect insects from predators.

proton A positive charge.

quadrilateral A four-sided polygon formed by four line segments.

radioactive decay The breaking apart of the nucleus of an atom.

radioactive element The condition of elements that have undergone radioactive decay.

radio waves A form of electromagnetic radiation.

reaction time The time it takes you to respond to a situation; such as how long it takes you to catch the falling stick.

rectangle A polygon made of four sides with two pairs of parallel sides and right angles.

reflect To bounce back from a surface.

relative age The age of an object or event as compared with that of another object or event.

reproduction Production of offspring.

research The process of collecting information and data about a topic being studied.

retina The back portion of the eye where images are projected.

revolve To move in a curved path about an object.

rhomboid A parallelogram that has no right angles and only opposite sides are congruent.

Richter scale A number system used to measure the total shaking energy of an earthquake.

right angle An angle that measures 90 degrees.

rock A solid made up of one or more minerals.

rock formers The abundant minerals that make up the bulk of the lithosphere.

roots Special organs that anchor a plant, absorb water and minerals, and, sometimes, store food.

rust Iron oxide, formed by the oxidation of iron.

saliva A digestive liquid.

sap The liquid in plants.

satellite A body that moves in a curved path about a celestial body.

scapula Shoulder blade.

science project An investigation using the scientific method to discover the answer to a scientific problem.

science research Information and/or data that someone else has collected.

scientific method The process of thinking through the possibilities of solutions to a problem and testing each possibility for the best solution.

seasons Periods of the year characterized by specific weather.

secondary research Information and/or data that someone else has collected.

sediment Weathered rock material that is transported by wind, water, or ice and then deposited.

seismology The study of earthquakes.

sensory receptors Cells that can detect differences in pressure and temperature due to their sensitivity to touch.

shear-wall bracing Solid walls over a frame.

shore The land at the shoreline.

shoreline The area where the ocean and the land meet.

solar eclipse When the Moon passes directly between the Sun and the Earth, blocking the light of the Sun from a viewer on Earth. The Earth, Moon, and Sun are directly in line.

solar energy Electromagnetic radiation; energy that is emitted by the Sun.

solid The phase of matter with a definite volume and shape.

sound Vibrations traveling through materials.

sources Places where information is obtained, such as from written materials and people.

south pole End of a free-swinging magnet, such as a compass needle, that points toward Earth's magnetic south pole.

spectrophotometer An instrument that determines the color of light that a substance, such as a pigment, absorbs and transmits.

starch A complex chemical in some foods.

static charges Stationary electric charges.

static discharge The loss of static charges.

static electricity Energy due to the buildup of static charges in one place; these electric charges can be positive or negative.

stationary Not moving.

stem A plant organ that supports other organs, such as leaves and flowers.

stimuli Things that cause a response in a living organism.

table A diagram that uses words and numbers in columns and rows to represent data.

tabular Table top in shape.

tarsus The fourth and outermost main section of an insect's leg.

temperature Measurement in degrees of how hot or cold a material is; the average energy of motion of the molecules in a material.

terrarium Closed container housing small plants and sometimes small animals such as snails, frogs, or snakes.

thermometer Instrument used to measure temperature.

thorax The middle part of an insect's body.

tibia The third main section of an insect's leg.

tissue A group of cells that perform a similar task.

topic research Research used to select a project topic.

topologically equivalent Figures that can be obtained from one another without cutting the figure or punching a hole.

topology The branch of geometry that studies properties of geometric figures that remain unchanged when the size or shape of the figures is gradually changed.

total solar eclipse When the moon passes in front of and blocks all of the Sun's light. Occurs when an observer is in the umbra of the Moon's shadow.

transmit To pass through a material.

transport To carry from one place to another.

trapezium A quadrilateral with no parallel sides.

trapezoid A quadrilateral with one pair of parallel sides.

triangle A polygon made of three sides; the sum of the angles created by the three sides is always 180 degrees.

umbra The darkest part of a shadow.

variable Something that has an effect on an experiment. See also **independent variable, dependent variable,** and **controlled variable.**

veins A framework of thickened ridges in an insect's wings.

vent Channel of a volcano that connects the source of magma to the volcano's opening.

vertex Point where two lines meet.

vertical Up-and-down direction.

vibrate To quickly move back and forth.

viscosity The measurement of a liquid's ability to flow.

visible light Light made up of colors that can be seen by the human eye, commonly referred to as rainbow colors: red, orange, yellow, green, blue, indigo, and violet.

volcano Opening in the Earth from which molten rock pours.

volcanology The study of volcanoes.

water vapor Water in its gas form.

water waves Disturbances on the surface of water that repeat themselves.

weather The result of changing conditions in Earth's atmosphere.

weathering The process by which rocks are broken into small pieces.

weather vane An instrument that shows wind direction.

wheel and axle A simple machine made up of a large wheel attached to a shaft called an axle. The wheel and axle turn together.

wind Movement of air in a general horizontal direction.

xylem tubes Tubes in plants that transport sap containing water and minerals from the roots throughout the plant.

zoology The study of animals, including their structure and growth.

Index

155